Bestselling books from UoLearn

How to develop
Your Assertive
Communication
UK 9781539391555
World 9781537637723

How to Write
Excellent Reports
UK 9781539381891
World 9781849370899

Speed Writing
Modern Shorthand
UK 9781537566603
World 9781532704918

Speed Writing
Dictionary
UK: 9781542302753
World: 9781542302777

How to Take
Minutes of Meetings
UK 9781539370376
World 9781532737602

Successful
Business Writing
UK 9781539381839
World 9781532737688

Order books from Amazon or your favourite
bookseller and from www.uolearn.com.

The Art of Influencing - How to Influence Effectively UK Spelling

The 7 traits of influential people and 6 steps to influence people by setting goals and outcomes, increasing your credibility, trustworthiness, empathy, creativity, communication, assertive, persuasion and influencing skills.

Published by: Universe of Learning Ltd,
Company reg number 6485477, Lancashire, UK
www.UoLearn.com, support@UoLearn.com

ISBN 978-1539391517

Other editions: world / US spelling 978-1537637785

Skills Training Course, Universe of Learning and UoLearn are trademarks of Universe of Learning Ltd.

Photographs © www.fotolia.com and adobe.com
Edited by Dr Margaret Greenhall.

What do people say about this book?

"Very readable book which has changed my perspective on influencing. I always thought of it as a set of tools and techniques, but the idea of becoming more influential is much more interesting. This book makes that idea feel possible".

"I liked the whole concept of developing the traits of influential people and really liked the way they were presented. I enjoyed the exercises and have started to influence people in different ways as a result. Thank you for the ideas."

"It has made me realise that perhaps I have put too much effort into influencing external clients and stakeholders and not enough time trying to be influential with my own staff!!"

"I quickly realised that influencing is a much broader topic than I had imagined. I gained from it an understanding that I stand a better chance of maximising my effectiveness if I play to my own strengths, rather than trying to meet others' expectations of me."

"Most importantly, I learnt that some of the "influencing" I see employed by others is really manipulations and not only is it not necessary but it can in fact be counterproductive to subscribe to this method. It was very reassuring to hear that I don't have to become someone I'm not in order to extend my influence!"

"An excellent and practical guide to the development of influencing skills. Written in an easy to understand way, it is highly readable and recommended."

"Useful, practical, informative. The information and exercises are set out clearly and succinctly. A really useful book that can be referred to as and when needed."

"I love the structure that the authors develop for influencing skills. The seven traits are well thought out and explained and provide a really solid basis for focussed self-development.

Much of the guidance then provided on improving the traits is common sense - but it is difficult to see how it wouldn't be! The book is also stuffed with exercises, many very good.

Overall this is a good book if you need to improve your influencing skills, or if you are a trainer in this area and want a fresh perspective on the topic.

It's a quick read and good value for money."

"This book is set out in such a clear, easy to read format, so that it is very easy to work through. I found that it engaged me with all the exercises, and I love the 'tips' that you can focus on as you work towards being a person who can influence without being a manipulative person!"

"At last! A personal development book without the jargon! I found it very easy to read and very believable. The layout of the book allows you to concentrate on areas of particular relevance - but I recommend you read the whole thing! The examples are relevant and helped me to understand how I can increase my influence in not only my professional, but also my personal life. I look forward to putting the ideas into action!"

About the authors:
Lois Burton and
Deborah Dalley

Deborah Dalley and Lois Burton both have their roots in the field of learning and development and both have over 25 years experience. They both run successful consultancy and coaching businesses and work on many collaborative projects as colleagues and friends.

With backgrounds that span work in the public, private and voluntary sectors, Lois and Deborah share many professional interests and values and bring complementary experience to their work.

Deborah and Lois have also written The Steps To Influencing, now included in this new edition. Both are deeply committed to developing the potential of leaders and managers and helping to create high performance teams.

Deborah Dalley

Deborah Dalley has been working as a freelance training and development consultant for over 25 years. Her employment background is in the Criminal Justice System and Higher Education. She has carved a niche as a primary consultant in the Higher Education sector in the North West of England. Deborah is particularly interested in leadership and team development in this sector with much of her work focusing around influencing, emotional intelligence and the management of change.

Deborah's areas of expertise include:

- ✓ Powerful influencing
- ✓ Happiness and motivation
- ✓ Assertive communication
- ✓ Emotional intelligence
- ✓ Leadership and management development
- ✓ Managing change and transition
- ✓ Team development

Deborah has been involved in numerous major organisational change initiatives and has worked with managers and leadership teams over many years. She brings this experience to bear in her work and has a passionate interest in helping managers to cope with the challenges that constant change brings.

Deborah has developed a powerful model for holding courageous conversations which helps to remove some of the blocks and barriers to effective communication within organisations.

Deborah is the best selling author of How to Develop Your Assertive Communication, UK 978-1539391555 and world 978-1537637723

Please contact Deborah at www.deborahdalley.com

Lois Burton

Lois is an innovative and progressive leadership development consultant and leadership coach whose career over the last 25 years has included work with many of the most complex issues for individuals and organisations. She is passionate about developing authentic, confident leaders who can fulfil their potential, build extraordinary teams, increase leadership capacity and create successful and resilient organisations.

Lois's areas of expertise include:

- ✓ Powerful influencing
- ✓ Leadership development
- ✓ Leadership and executive coaching
- ✓ Leadership team coaching
- ✓ Positive psychology
- ✓ Development of emotional intelligence
- ✓ Developing a mindset for success
- ✓ Coach training

She also specialises in coaching exceptional senior leadership teams and in personal and organisational change.

Lois is an accredited consultant and coach in emotional intelligence for Hay Group Worldwide and is also accredited with the Barrett Values Centre for the use of their tools for corporate transformation.

Lois runs intensive leadership retreats and senior leadership programmes based on coaching principles, and developing communities of leadership learning. She is currently working on a programme to help leaders develop the mindset for success.

Please contact Lois at www.loisburton.co.uk

Contents

What do people say about this book   **3**

About the authors   **5**

Part 1: The Art of Influencing   11

Introduction: The art of influencing   12

Who is this book for?   13
How to use this book   14
What are the 7 traits?   15
The difference between influence and manipulation   17

Trait 1: Knowing what you want and believing you can achieve it   20

Sense of purpose and clear outcomes   21
Believing you can achieve your desired outcomes   30
Self belief   31
Taking risks   34
Resilience   36
Summary of trait 1   38

Trait 2: Credibility   40

Increasing your credibility   44
Building your reputation   45
Developing your expertise   46
Improving your ability to deliver   47
Summary of trait 2   50

Trait 3: Trustworthiness 52

Authenticity 54
Intent 62
Behaviours that generate trust 63
Developing your trustworthiness 66
Summary of trait 3 68

Trait 4: Empathy 70

Maps of the world – exploring other points of view 72
The skills of empathising 73
Insightful questioning 73
Active listening 75
Developing your empathy 77
Summary of trait 4 80

Trait 5: Inspirational 82

What do we mean by inspirational? 82
Inspiring yourself 83
Inspiring others 89
Tips for inspiring other people 90
Summary of trait 5 94

Trait 6: Strong communication capability 96

The elements of a strong communication capability 98
Verbal impact 99
Ability to structure verbal communication with logic 100
Contextualising your language 102
Avoiding unhelpful language patterns 104
Ability to structure insightful questions and to listen well 106
Non-verbal impact 107
Voice projection and great use of emphasis and tone 108
Image and personal presentation 109
Congruence 111
Written impact 114
Impact in presentations 116
Summary of trait 6 118

Trait 7: Open-mindedness   **120**

How open-minded are you?   121
What gets in the way of being open-minded?   123
Negative thinking   123
Habit   124
Developing flexible thinking   126
Considering other viewpoints   128
PACE technique   128
Seeking feedback   129
Summary of trait 7   134
Answers to puzzles   178

Personal action plan   **135**

Part 2: A Step by Step Guide to Influencing Effectively   **137**

Introduction to the Six Steps   **138**

Step 1: Defining what you want   **140**

Step 2: Assessing the views of others   **142**

Step 3: Defining our influencing power   **146**

Step 4: Communicating appropriately   **152**

Step 5: Provide space for discussion, questions and feedback **154**

Step 6: Concluding   **156**

Conclusion to the steps   **160**

The six steps case studies   **161**

Final thoughts   **176**

Part 1:
The Art of Influencing

"Influence is not only held by people in authority;
any one of us can learn to become more
influential in our lives and work."

Lois Burton and Deborah Dalley

Introduction: The art of influencing

When you think of someone influential who comes to mind?

Is it famous names like Nelson Mandela, Emmeline Pankhurst, Christine Lagarde, Bill Gates – people who are on the global stage affecting the world, or is it someone you know at work – a chief executive, director, manager or leader in your organisation? Is it a teacher, doctor, carer – someone who powerfully affects your life at a deeper level or indeed a member of your family or a friend – someone who makes your life better? Or do you think of yourself?

We all have our own ideas about who we see as being influential, but what characteristics make these people stand out?
The answer to the above question is what the first section of this book is all about.

For the last twenty five years we have worked with individuals and groups looking at the skills of influencing. As we have worked with people on this topic two key lessons have emerged:

Firstly, the notion that becoming more influential is more than picking up a set of specific influencing tools and techniques.

Secondly, that there are certain traits that influential people have in common and these can be developed.

Who is this book for?

This book has been written with several audiences in mind – it can be used by:

- ✓ Individuals who are interested in assessing and developing their personal influence

- ✓ Learning professionals who want to use the exercises with groups in their training sessions

- ✓ Managers or coaches who can use many of the exercises to help an individual to think through ways to increase their influence

- ✓ Managers who want to develop a more influential leadership style

The first part of this book will explain what those traits are. We will describe each of the traits, provide case studies and exercises to enable you to explore and reflect on these traits and help you to develop your personal action plan to becoming more influential.

The second part of this book is about understanding how to fully prepare yourself using six steps to influence the outcome in a specific situation. This is a stand alone set of tools that can be used without necessarily having completed the work on the traits.

How to use this book

Part one - the 7 traits

Following the introductory chapter, this section is divided into seven parts. Each chapter covers one of the traits and aims to:

➢ Describe the trait and help you to recognise whether you currently demonstrate those behaviours

➢ Provide guidance, case studies and exercises on ways to develop the characteristics of each trait further

There is no particular order to the traits so you can use this book in any way that you want. Work through all seven traits or dip in at any point that interests you.

At the end of each chapter we have listed a number of websites and books that you may find useful for further reading. At the end of part 1 there is an action plan. You can record any thoughts about personal actions to become more influential.

If you visit our website, www.UoLearn.com, then you will find a free downloadable workbook with all the exercises from this section and plenty of space to make your own notes.

Part two- the 6 steps

In this part of the book we will outline a structured six step process to use when you have a particular situation where you want to influence the outcome.

Each step is explained with exercises to help you to prepare your case to influence. There are two longer case studies at the end to help you understand how to use the six steps.

What are the 7 traits?

Over the years we have worked in the field of personal development, it has become increasingly evident that influencing is not an exact science, it is an art. It is not a set of manipulative tools and techniques that can be learned on a one day course. It is a way of being – a set of beliefs and behaviours that are evident in the way an individual conducts both their professional and private lives.

We have identified seven traits that are shared by influential people:

- ➢ **Knowing what you want and believing that you can get it**
  Being clear about our sense of purpose and outcomes is the first step to becoming more influential.

- ➢ **Credibility**
  This is about how believable we are to other people. Our credibility with someone comes from three things: the reputation we have' how they perceive our expertise and what has happened in the past.

- ➢ **Trustworthiness**
  This is a fundamental element of influence. We are more open to be influenced by someone that we trust and we are more inclined to trust people we think are authentic. This is often described as being the same on the outside as on the inside. The most influential leaders are those who operate from values such as truth, trust and integrity and use those values with the intent to benefit not just themselves but the people around them as well.

➢ **Empathy**
It is important to remember that we will never influence someone from our point of view. The ability to step away from our personal viewpoint and explore someone else's perception of the world is essential.

➢ **Inspirational**
Enthusiasm is infectious. We have all experienced how contagious negative emotion can be and it is equally true of positive energy. Inspiring others involves motivating and capturing their imagination. Martin Luther King used powerful imagery in his famous "I have a dream" speech – the picture he painted and the feelings it evoked did far more to capture the imagination and influence others than a factual account would have done.

➢ **Strong Communication Capability**
However self aware, genuine and honest we are, the ability to get others to follow comes from our capacity to communicate effectively. Highly influential people are usually articulate, willing and able to listen and often charismatic. They are also aware of their impact and the effect they have on others.

➢ **Open-Mindedness**
Flexibility and a willingness to embrace change are also traits that are evident in most influential people.

Open-mindedness
Knowing what you want
Communication capability
7 traits
Credibility
Inspirational
Trustworthiness
Empathy

The difference between influence and manipulation

We want to start by clarifying the differences between becoming more influential and influencing by manipulation.

Does becoming more influential mean becoming an expert in the art of manipulating others to get what you want? In our experience as training providers, this is the question that we have often debated with our delegates.

This question creates a tension in many people as they don't want to feel manipulative, however, they do want to feel able to both convince and persuade others. It doesn't help that many role models seen as being influential both in organisational and public life are also seen as manipulative – masters of spin. The other difficulty is that many people see these tactics working for those who use them and have few examples of other ways of influencing that are equally successful.

We are looking to show a different way for those who wish to become more influential but do not wish to become more manipulative. Our intention is firstly, to challenge the premise that manipulation truly succeeds in any sustainable way and to look at the differences between influence and manipulation.

Manipulation is defined as:
"To manage or control artfully or by shrewd use of influence, often in an unfair or fraudulent way."

By contrast, influence is defined as:
"A power affecting a person, thing, or course of events, especially one that operates without any direct or apparent effort."

It is very clear within these definitions that manipulation, whilst seen as shrewd, also has the elements of unfairness and fraudulence within it whilst influence is concerned with a powerful effect but does not need to carry the darker side of manipulation within it.

Some of the influencing tactics and techniques we have seen taught on training courses can appear to be effective in the short term, however, they often carry inherent pitfalls because they can be seen as being manipulative.

So what are those pitfalls?

First and foremost, there may be a loss of self-confidence and trust in yourself. If you are constantly looking for ways to win in situations, then you focus only on undermining the views of others and lose your sense of integrity and identity in the process. If you look at some of the public figures who have been caught in manipulative practices, all have eventually become run by their own fear and insecurity and in the process have lost their confidence and thus their power and impact. Some recover, but many never do.

Secondly, you may lose the confidence and trust of others. At work and at home we are often trying to influence the same people time and time again. If someone feels that you have tried to manipulate them or outmanoeuvre them in the past then the trust between you will be diminished. Trust takes a long time to build but can be lost in a moment. Once lost, it takes even longer to build again and without it our capacity to influence that person is significantly reduced.

Thirdly, the loss of the end goal. Machiavelli propounded the principle that the end justifies the means. This is the seduction that leads many down the manipulative path – if I am looking at an end that is inherently right, am I not justified in a little manipulation to get there? Time and time again this has been proven to be a false principle – the means nearly always impact the end goal and an end goal gained by manipulation never maintains its original integrity.

Trait 1:

Knowing what you want and believing you can achieve it.

"Believe and act as if it were impossible to fail."

Charles Kettering

Trait 1:

Knowing what you want and believing you can achieve it

In this section we will be:

✓ Defining the trait

✓ Clarifying the importance of developing a strong sense of purpose and clear outcomes

✓ Explaining the importance of articulating those outcomes in a positive way, i.e. saying what you want as opposed to what you don't want!

✓ Exploring how to build your belief in your ability to achieve your goals through developing self-belief, considered risk taking and resilience

"Let him who would move the world, first move himself." Socrates

What do we mean by knowing what you want and believing you can achieve it?

It is important to define our starting point. An initial trait which we believe is fundamental to influential people is knowing what you want AND believing you are going to get it.

What we mean by this is, a strong sense of purpose, clarity around the outcomes needed to achieve your purpose and an equally strong belief in your ability to achieve it. These are the building blocks to increasing your influence. All of the influential people we have observed exhibit this trait.

Sense of purpose and clear outcomes

There are hundreds (probably thousands) of books and tapes on self-development that stress the importance of clear outcomes and goals. What we have observed in highly influential people is that they not only have clarity around these outcomes – they also have a clearly defined sense of purpose. This gives them a direction and context in which to operate. Having a defined sense of purpose gives energy and meaning to your goals. This is the reason that we are including both within this book – we see these as the twin foundation stones to developing your influencing skills.

Other people respond to this clear and deep seated sense of purpose and outcomes.

One of the reasons this is so attractive is that many of us find defining our sense of purpose and creating clarity around outcomes quite challenging. Often we have been defined by other people's expectations and have never really connected to our own.

We have worked with many people over the years who have struggled to identify what they are really trying to achieve.

*"If you don't know where you are going
you will probably end up somewhere else."*
Laurence Peter

Some common dilemmas that people have brought to training sessions or coaching include:

➢ Do I want to be the best teacher/lawyer/nurse in the profession and practise my craft
   or do I want to manage the process and move up through the organisation?

➢ Do I know what I want from my life
   or do I follow the things that others expect from me?

➢ Do I work to live
   or live to work?

➢ Do I want to influence this decision because it will be good for my career
   or because I truly believe it is the right thing to do?

Do any of these sound familiar?

If you are struggling with this type of dilemma, then it directly impacts your ability to set outcomes with any sense of clarity. You are unable to decide which is the right direction or will be trying subconsciously to meet two different and sometimes conflicting sets of outcomes. Developing a sense of purpose can be seen as slightly removed from the pragmatic world of work that most of us operate in. However, we believe that the lack of purpose is one of most common reasons for lack of influence and working on this area can dramatically increase your capacity to become more influential.

The starting point to build a foundation from which to influence is to ask yourself, "What do I really want to happen and for what reason?" This can relate to our lives as a whole or to a particular area in which we want to influence the outcome.

In order to do this, we have to acknowledge that we have both the right and responsibility to take control of our own lives rather than being defined by other people's expectations. Influential people are not defined by others, they forge their own path.

Tips to develop a clear sense of purpose and set specific outcomes:

✓ **Be prepared to spend time on this** – many people when asked what they want to happen, say "I don't know, I've never known, things just happen, don't they, and then you make the best of them." This is simply not good enough. If you want to influence what happens in your life and career then you need to be prepared to spend time working out those outcomes as you would work on any plan.

✓ **Get help** – there are numerous books and exercises devoted solely to clarity of outcome and goal setting. If you cannot do this alone, get a coach who can work with you.

✓ **Start small if you are struggling** – this is a direct contradiction to some of the advice on goal setting which says always look at whatever your overall life goals are and work back from there. Much of the evidence now says that the paradigm of setting big life goals is faulty and therefore, it's much better to have clarity around purpose and define your outcomes in smaller ways to start with, expanding as you go. So start in a small way and work up.

Case Study

One of the delegates on the training course started with what he enjoyed in his current job and would not want to lose. We looked at a very specific area based on his next job containing opportunities to do more research and less teaching.

He then decided his first desired outcome was to have a conversation with his manager to see if he could adjust the balance slightly in his current role to prepare him better for the next step. He achieved this within a fortnight, which then gave him the confidence to move onto saying that his ultimate goal was to do research full time, which would fulfil his sense of purpose and also to develop a working pattern that gave him more flexibility so he could do more work from home and travel less for work. He set a two year time span for this and from there had conversations which started to push him in the right direction. This example of starting small meant that this delegate could move onto the bigger picture as a result, whereas in that first session, he simply could not envision the bigger picture.

Exercise: Creating clear desired outcomes

Think about your current job (or situation if you do not currently have a job).
What is it that you most enjoy at the moment?
What would you like more of?

Identify one action that will help you get more of what you enjoy and state it as a desired outcome, i.e.

My goal is to create more

....
....
....
....
....
....

in my job or current situation.

Next, identify one action that will influence that goal and bring it nearer.

My action is

....
....
....
....
....

I commit to taking this action by

....

Once you have achieved one desired outcome, it gives you the confidence to go on from there. Do this exercise again once you have achieved your first outcome and start to expand your horizons. You are on the path to becoming more influential in your own life and with others.

Articulating your desired outcomes in a positive way

Getting clear on what you want is one thing, articulating those goals is different again. It is surprising just how many people when asked what they want are less than clear in their reply.

From our experience, it is much easier for people to say what they don't want rather than what they do. Stating your desired outcomes in the negative, i.e. from the perspective of what you don't want is not an influential trait. It creates a negative impression and is also frustrating – to become more influential it is essential that your starting point is clarity about what you do want.

It is very easy to start your influencing in the wrong way if you have not defined what you want in the first place.

Consider the following case study which was brought forward as an influencing problem in a coaching session.

Case Study

The coachee was one of 3 senior team leaders in a high profile department, which was undergoing a restructure.

Her starting point was:

My department is undergoing a restructure and I want to influence how my team is structured. At present, I am not part of the decision making group although one of my colleagues, who is a team leader in exactly the same position as I am, is part of the group. I feel very frustrated by this situation.

I have told my boss that I don't want my team to be structured in exactly the same way as my colleagues as we have a different role and need a different structure. I think it could be a real problem and I am worried about it. What I think could happen is that decisions will be made which are not right for my team and what I don't want is for that to happen and we then have to start unpicking those decisions.

All my boss said to me was that I didn't need to worry because the needs of all the different teams will be taken into consideration by the decision making group but he appreciated my concern and would make sure that this point was reinforced.

This was not the response I wanted at all. I feel even more frustrated now because I still think that my concerns are justified and I don't believe that anyone who doesn't work in the team will have a full understanding of what we need.

Does this ring any bells for you?

This is an all too familiar scenario from which someone starts their influencing process by stating what they don't want rather than what they do want and inevitably gets the response they don't want! Talking about what you don't want invites confusion, as in the above scenario.

Her manager was completely unclear about what she wanted. The manager answered what he assumed was the question he had been asked.

I.e. "How will the decisions be made and can I be sure that my team's role will be taken into consideration?"

Actually the question was, "May I be part of the decision making group as I believe that my contribution would be vital to ensuring my team is structured in the right way?"

Feel the difference when someone starts with what they do want and frames the request clearly. This is not to say that the first answer you get will always be the one you want. However, at least you start in the right place.

Influential people always start in the right place. They are not afraid to ask for what they want clearly and directly. You are then in the position to build on that.

In this instance we worked on how this coachee could set up another conversation in which she clarified with her manager what she wanted. It worked. Her manager had assumed that the coachee was too busy to be part of the group and had therefore given the role to her colleague whose workload was slightly less. After a much more constructive discussion, both she and the third team leader were invited to be part of the decision making group.

Exercise: How clearly do you state your desired outcomes?

Think about a situation in which you want to influence more strongly:-

First, write down the present situation and the way(s) you have been dealing with it, being as honest as you can so that you can check if you are falling into the "don't want" trap.

....

....

....

....

....

....

Secondly, write down your goal/exactly what you want out of the situation as clearly as possible.

....

....

....

....

....

....

Make sure that you have written your goals in a positive way - have you stated what you want?

You now have your starting point!

Practise this skill in all situations in which you want to increase your influence. You must be clear at the outset to have any chance of influencing strongly.

Believing you can achieve your desired outcomes

Influential people not only know what they want,
they believe strongly in their own ability to get it.

There are 3 parts to strengthening your belief in your ability to achieve your goals:

✓ **Self-belief**

✓ **Considered risk taking**

✓ **Resilience**

Influential people understand the importance of believing in themselves. They also have a willingness to step out of their comfort zones, to take some risks and have the resilience to bounce back from setbacks. We rarely achieve our goals without meeting some obstacles.

Influential people hold onto their goals in the face of setbacks and have the resilience to get straight back in the game.

Self-belief

It sounds self evident, but what is self-belief and how do we foster it?

Self-belief is the inner confidence that you will succeed and that you can overcome obstacles to achieve your goals.

How can we foster our self-belief?
Focusing on the best rather than the worst is the key.

Exercise: Successful times

Make a list of all the times you have successfully influenced situations in your life.

....

....

....

....

....

....

Write down what you did that helped that process:

....

....

....

....

....

....

Keep that list easily accessible so that you can focus on those occasions rather than on times when you have been unsuccessful. Focusing on our best times rather than our worst times helps to foster self-belief.

We can strengthen our self-belief by the willingness to focus on positive characteristics rather than negative and acknowledging the fact that our own negative self talk, our inner critic is the biggest enemy of our self-belief. When we listen too strongly to our inner critic it saps our self-belief and paralyses our ability to believe that we can achieve our goals. As with the don't want trap, there is also a won't get trap!

Another enemy of self-belief is fear of failure, which we explore in more detail in the risk taking section. Because we fear failure many people will not try in the first place. The faulty thinking goes something like this, "It's not worth trying because I probably won't succeed and if I don't succeed when I have tried really hard then I will feel worse than I do now!"

Many people will not take action/ask for what they want because they make the assumption that they will not get it, therefore there is no point in asking. This saves them from having to face up to a potential set back, which often gets labelled as failure. Yet, few people succeed in anything important the first time – influential people accept this and cultivate the resilience to deal with it. On being asked about how it felt to fail so many times when he was working on the invention of the light bulb, Thomas Edison said:

"I have not failed 700 times. I have not failed once. I have succeeded in proving that those 700 ways will not work. When I have eliminated the ways that will not work, I will find the way that will work."

Beware not only of the "don't want" mindset but of the "won't get" mindset. Won't get becomes a self-fulfilling prophecy - we assume we won't get, therefore, we don't ask or we ask in the wrong way, therefore we don't get, therefore our self-belief goes down and next time we make the same assumption of won't get from an even more negative mindset. This drains our influence completely.

If you take the previous case study as an example, that person had assumed that there was some kind of problem with her belonging to the group. She did not know the real reason, so built her own fantasy that there was no point in asking directly, as obviously she wouldn't get the right answer. She therefore asked the wrong question and her self-fulfilling prophecy came true.

We have to break the mindset of won't get to increase our influence!

Our won't get (don't deserve to get) voice sounds something like this:

- ✗ My needs are not as important as theirs.
- ✗ They won't like my ideas.
- ✗ Should I say something or will that look as if I am interfering?
- ✗ If it doesn't work out it will look as though I have failed.
- ✗ I will feel really embarrassed if others do not agree.
- ✗ Maybe I am wrong.
- ✗ It will be an uphill battle to get others to agree and I'm not sure if I have the energy.

In order to combat our won't get voice, we have to be able to access thoughts that create a will get mindset. The will get mindset is at the heart of self-belief.

Our will get voice sounds something like this:

- ✓ I value my needs as much as the needs of others.
- ✓ I know my ideas are good and I believe other people will think so too.
- ✓ I want to help and therefore, I need to say something.
- ✓ If it doesn't work out – at least I know I have tried.
- ✓ If others don't agree we can talk about it – it means I will have opened up the dialogue.
- ✓ What if I'm right?
- ✓ This is important to me, therefore, I know I will find the energy to influence others and I do have lots of support to draw on.
- ✓ If at first you don't succeed......................
- ✓ I know I can achieve this – I just need to find the right way to go about it.

Imagine, focus, believe and keep going!

Taking risks

The ability to develop a will get mindset does mean that we have to be prepared to take some risks. Risk is part of growth. If we look at truly influential people in the world they have all been willing to follow their vision and goals even if that has involved an element of risk. Very few people succeed without taking risks and learning from setbacks. One of the problems with an increasingly litigious culture is that we strive to eliminate risk. This can and often does paralyse people – we have watched many managers lose the belief and loyalty of their staff because they have become unable to take a decision. We have to be able to step out of our comfort zone and live with a degree of uncertainty.

Taking calculated risks is very different from acting rashly. It is about accepting that sometimes we have to take action without being totally sure that nothing can go wrong or be lost.

To laugh is to risk appearing the fool.
To weep is to risk appearing sentimental.
To reach out to another is to risk involvement.
To expose feelings is to risk exposing your true self.
To place your dreams, ideas before a crowd is to risk their loss.
To love is to risk not being loved in return.
To live is to risk dying. To hope is to risk despair.
To try is to risk failure.
But risks must be taken, because the greatest hazard in life is to risk nothing.
The person who risks nothing, does nothing, has nothing and is nothing.
They may avoid suffering and sorrow, but they cannot learn, feel, change, grow, love, live.
Chained by their certitudes, they are a slave:
they have forfeited their freedom.
Only a person who risks is truly free.   *[unattributed]*

As we discussed earlier in self-belief, fear is behind most of our difficulties with taking risks. Many fears are irrational but nonetheless very real and difficult to overcome. Starting to deal with our fears is an essential element of being able to take the right amount of risk.

Exercise:
Avoiding being trapped by irrational fears and beliefs

Identify an occasion when you felt unable to try something different or take a risk and then identify what you were afraid might happen as a result. Was this a rational fear or an irrational one? E.g. I wanted to introduce a new system at work but was afraid I would look foolish if it didn't work.

This type of fear is very common and you need to challenge the idea that you will look foolish. It is often more foolish not to try a new idea and if you have thought it out thoroughly many people will applaud you for trying to improve something. Doing nothing does not serve you or increase your influence.

Identify an occasion like this from your own experience.

Occasion when I felt unable to take a risk:

....

....

....

What I was afraid might happen as a result:

....

....

....

Challenge the fear that was behind your inability to take a risk and see if you can reframe it for yourself. Write down what you will do differently next time – if you are struggling with this have a look at the tips at the end of this chapter or try reading a book on building self-confidence.
What will I do differently next time?

....

....

....

Resilience

To be resilient means to be able to "spring back" into shape. To be emotionally resilient means to be able to spring back emotionally after suffering through difficult and stressful times in one's life. Stressed people experience a flood of powerful negative emotions which may include anger, anxiety, and depression. Some people remain trapped in these negative emotions long after the stressful events that have caused them have passed. Emotionally resilient people, on the other hand, are quickly able to bounce back to their normal emotional state.

Resilience and the ability to bounce back from setbacks is another aspect of believing you can achieve your goals. Few people achieve their goals immediately, and those who throw in their hand after a setback diminish their influence. If your self-belief is strong this strengthens your resilience and increases your chance of success. All of the most influential figures in history have recognised the importance of resilience and practised it.

When Thomas Edison's factory was burned down with much of his work lost, he said:

"There is a great value in disaster. All our mistakes are burned up. Thank God we can start anew."

Increasing your influence also means increasing your resilience.

Tips to build your resilience and self-belief:

✓ List 3 reasons why your views are valued and valuable.
✓ Create a support network that can help and encourage you; cheerleaders are very important.
✓ Combat stress, stress is the enemy of resilience.
✓ Read motivational books and articles.
✓ Watch motivational films.
✓ Avoid "awfulising" – letting your thoughts about how awful you or the situation are to spiral out of control.
✓ List all the positive things about yourself (we tend to dwell on the negative).
✓ If other people praise you, accept it as genuine.
✓ Practise visualising success, not failure.
✓ Use positive language
  ‣ I will...... not I should
  ‣ I am going to.........not I will try to
  ‣ I could if............not I can't because
✓ Congratulate yourself when things go well.
✓ If you have a problem that you can do something about, do it – if you cannot do anything about it then incorporate it into your plans rather than keep wishing that it was different.
✓ Acknowledge and learn from your mistakes but do not spend a lot of time or energy blaming yourself or others.

Exercise: Your support network

List your support network – include only people who foster your self belief rather than undermine you.

....

....

....

If your list is quite small, think about how you could expand your support network, e.g. join a club or business network. List your ideas:

....

....

....

Summary of trait 1:
Knowing what you want and believing that you can achieve it

In summary, to develop this trait concentrate on:

✓ Developing your sense of purpose and clarifying your goals, remember to start small if you are struggling

✓ Avoid defining yourself by the expectations of others

✓ Articulate your outcomes and goals clearly

✓ Focus on what you do want not what you don't want. Avoid the "don't want" trap

✓ Remember Edison – cultivate resilience

✓ Build a strong support network

✓ Beat the "won't get" mindset: it is totally possible to change a mindset

✓ Be willing to step out of your comfort zone and take a risk

Further Reading:

Feel the Fear and Do It Anyway, Susan Jeffers, Vermillion, 978-0091907075

The Self Esteem Workbook, Lynda Field, Vermillion, 978-0091857332

The Success Principles, Jack Canfield, William Morrow, 978-0062364289

www.businessballs.com/goal_planning.htm

www.valuescentre.com

Trait 2:
Credibility

"We judge ourselves by what we feel capable of doing,
while others judge us by what we have already done."

Henry Longfellow

Trait 2:
Credibility

In this section we will be:

✓ Defining what credibility means

✓ Examining how to assess your credibility rating with people

✓ Exploring how your reputation may affect your credibility

✓ Identifying ways to build your reputation

✓ Listing ways to develop your expertise and capability in order to be more credible

✓ Helping you to develop your ability to deliver what you promise

"The more you are willing to accept responsibility for your actions, the more credibility you will have." Brian Koslow

What is credibility?

Credibility is a critical element in how influential we are.
It is quite a difficult thing to define so let's begin with several dictionary definitions:

"The quality, capability or power to elicit belief."
"The quality of being believable and trustworthy."
"A reputation impacting on one's ability to be believed."

These definitions clearly demonstrate that credibility is not something we can assess about ourselves. It is something that other people perceive about us.

Exercise: Who do you think is credible?

Spend a few minutes identifying someone you know who you consider to be credible.

....

What are the key things about that person that made you choose them?

....
....
....
....
....

Some examples that people have given when answering this question include:

"I have identified my doctor as someone I consider to be credible. This is because I respect the knowledge and experience that she has and I have had very good advice from her in the past."

"My first manager stands out for me – he was always honest and open with me and if he said he was going to do something he did."

"I think the professor I work for is very credible – he is an expert in his field and has published many books. You often see his name quoted in things like the Lancet."

Your answer may not be the same as these, however, it probably does relate to at least one of the following:

> The capability of the individual
> The relationship you have with the person
> What other people have told you about them
> Their reputation
> Their qualifications or experience
> What has happened in the past between you and them

41

The key is to recognise that credibility can be developed. It might take some work, but it can be done. Invest your time and energy in doing the things that will achieve that, not in concentrating on things that you cannot do anything about. The following case study demonstrates how sometimes we lose sight of the things that we can actively do to increase our credibility.

Case Study

Sarah was a 28 year old graduate who had been working for the organisation for about 3 months. She was extremely energetic and I had been very impressed with the contribution she had made to the team. During her first personal development review I asked her how well she felt she had settled into the organisation. She said that she was finding it very difficult to work in such a male-dominated environment. She felt that people beyond the team did not take her seriously because she was young and female. She cited several examples of meetings in which she believed she had failed to influence the outcome because people did not believe she was old enough to be credible. We discussed the effect this was having on her work and she admitted that she was investing a lot of energy and time in dwelling on the unfairness of that perception. This had resulted in her becoming quite defensive and not contributing as much as she had when first appointed.

She quickly recognised that this was not a particularly productive path to follow and so decided to harness that time and energy in doing things that would increase her credibility. She began to build strong relationships within the organisation, establish a reputation for delivering results and spent a lot of time on her own personal development.
A year later Sarah was promoted!

This is a very common story. We often connect others' perception of our credibility to an issue that we cannot do anything about such as age, gender or educational background. It is undoubtedly true that some organisational cultures do attach credibility to things like experience or length of service. However, dwelling on these causes us to develop a victim status. It is important to recognise how destructive this is. If I am willing to accept that a group of people will not listen to me because I am female, or because of some other factor I cannot alter, then this will quickly become a self-fulfilling prophecy.

How credible we are comes essentially from three things:

> our expertise
> our reputation
> our track record with someone

It is important to differentiate between reputation in the wider world and direct experience of someone. How often have you heard people say things like, "Well loads of people complain about her but she has always been really helpful when I have asked her for something." If we establish a reputation for knowing what we are talking about, being honest, and delivering what we promise then our ability to elicit belief in others grows.

Increasing your credibility

As previously mentioned,, it is tricky to assess your own credibility because it is not something we can tell about ourselves. However, it can be useful to stop and think about the person you are trying to influence and try to gauge what they think about you – the following questions can help you to do that.

What is this person likely to know about my reputation?

➤ Where will they have heard my name mentioned?
➤ Who is likely to have talked to them about me?
➤ Do we share any acquaintances/work colleagues?
➤ What would they find out if they searched the internet?

What experience has this person had of dealing with me?

➤ Have I tried to influence them in the past?

If our credibility rating is low with an individual we are going to have to work much harder to influence them successfully.

Developing your credibility is not something that can be done overnight. It does take work. However there is no doubt that people are more likely to be influenced by someone that they consider credible, so the work does get rewarded! The following exercises will help you to think of ways to improve the three key components of increasing your credibility:

✓ **Your reputation**

✓ **Your expertise**

✓ **Your ability to deliver**

Building your reputation

All the things that have been discussed so far in this chapter rely on people knowing enough about you to make a decision about your credibility. A key area you can therefore work on in becoming more influential is building and developing your reputation.

Tips for building your reputation:

➢ Go to conferences and training courses and meet a variety of people.
➢ Offer to present at conferences and meetings.
➢ Prepare well for meetings and research what to talk about.
➢ Join online discussion groups.
➢ Use social media and digital communications strategically. Develop your profiles and keep them up to date, be proactive and direct people to meaningful content, don't just focus on trivia. Join the conversations that matter in your field, blog/vlog and guest on others blogs/vlogs, use Facebook live, build your followers and connections in a thoughtful way, connect to people who enhance your credibility, and finally, make sure you don't put anything on social media that will decrease your credibility.
➢ Keep in touch - send interesting articles or links to people.
➢ Focus on other people's needs – do things for others without expecting anything in return.
➢ Offer to join project groups.
➢ Arrive at meetings a bit early to talk to people.
➢ Don't just send an email – phone or arrange to meet.
➢ Write articles for in-house publications.
➢ Publicise your good work.
➢ Present the image of a positive thinker.

Exercise: Building your reputation

Identify three things you are going to do to build your reputation at work:

1
2
3

Developing your expertise

There are many activities both at work and in life that can provide opportunities for learning. When we think about ways to develop our knowledge and skills, we are often only consider courses and other formal development routes.

The following list highlights ways that we can learn new skills:

- Training courses both physical and virtual
- Reading
- Elearning and Massive Open Online Courses (MOOCs)
- Internet research
- Communities of practice and learning
- Conferences
- Coaching and mentoring
- Delegation
- Job rotation
- Secondment
- Job shadowing
- Giving presentations
- Deputising
- Sitting on project groups
- Magazines, trade and scholarly journals
- Relevant exhibitions
- Evening classes
- Attending meetings
- Chairing meetings
- Reports
- Videos, downloads and podcasts
- Project work
- Action learning and thinking groups
- Networking

Exercise: Your expertise

What other activities have you used to develop yourself over the past 2 years?

Exercise: Developing your expertise

Think about an area of knowledge or skill that you would like to develop. This could be work related or something you would like to do outside work. Once you have identified the area for development decide how you are going to meet that need.

Examples:
I would like to develop better time management skills.
I am going to do this by:

> Talking to and observing my line manager who is excellent at managing her time
> Buying a book on time management that has been recommended to me
> Attending the organisation's half day time management course

I would like to learn to speak French.
I am going to do this by:

> Choosing an online course
> Attending an evening French speaking class
> Hiring a tutor
> Arranging to speak conversational French with a French speaker

Choose an activity that you think will really enhance your expertise:

I would like to:

....

I am going to do this by:

....

....

....

....

Improving your ability to deliver

However strong your reputation and expertise are, it is still not enough if you do not do what you say you will.

As FedEx famously stated –
"A promise is nothing until it is delivered."

What stops you from delivering?

This is a question we have asked in many training workshops and the reasons given are varied. These have included:

- ✗ "Other people have not provided me with information I need to get the job done."
- ✗ "I do not have the right equipment to do the job properly so I won't do it at all."
- ✗ "I didn't have enough time."
- ✗ "I did not really understand what was expected."
- ✗ "I don't like doing things like this."
- ✗ "I need someone to help me with it."
- ✗ "If it goes wrong people will judge me."

It is important to concentrate on ways to overcome these obstacles by focusing on what we could have done differently rather than looking for things or people to blame!

Exercise: Improving your ability to deliver

Think about the last time you did not manage to deliver a task or project on time – what were the reasons?

....

....

....

What could you have done differently?

....

....

....

Tips to develop your time and project management skills:

✓ Develop systems to plan, organise and prioritise your work. This could include to do lists, effective diary management, year planners and filing systems.

✓ Know when you have the most energy during the day and plan to do the hardest tasks then. Most people are at their mental and physical best in the morning.

✓ Learn to say no to jobs that are not yours.

✓ Develop your skills in areas such as speed reading and report writing.

✓ Look at your to do list each day and tackle the thing that you are resisting the most first. Once you have done that task, everything else seems easier in comparison!

✓ Restrict interruptions by fixing time limits, meeting in the other person's office or remaining standing during the conversation.

✓ Break projects down into manageable parts and then set yourself interim deadlines. This helps to keep larger tasks moving forward.

Summary of trait 2: Credibility

In summary, to develop this trait, concentrate on:

✓ Thinking about ways to develop your reputation within the organisation and the wider community

✓ Ensuring that your expertise is up to date and that you are constantly growing and developing

✓ Implementing systems and processes that ensure that you can deliver what you have promised on time

Further Reading:

Get Everything Done and Still Have Time to Play, Mark Forster, Hodder and Stoughton, 978-0340746202

The Mind Gym: Give Me Time, Time Warner, 978-0316731690

Project Management Pocketbook, Keith Posner and Mike Applegarth, Pocketbooks, 978-1903776872

How to be a Productivity Ninja, Graham Alcott, Icon Books Ltd 978-1785780288

www.cipd.co.uk

Trait 3:
Trustworthiness

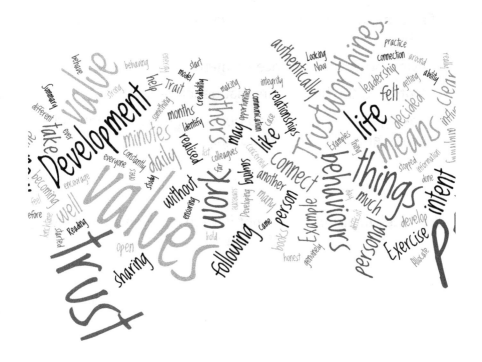

"When people honour each other, there is a trust established that leads to synergy, interdependence and deep respect. Both parties make decisions and choices based on what is right, what is best and what is valued most highly." Blaine Lee

Trait 3:
Trustworthiness

In this section we will be:

✓ Defining what trustworthiness means

✓ Examining why authenticity is an important element of trust

✓ Exploring how knowing what we value helps us to be more authentic

✓ Reviewing the importance of intent

✓ Identifying the behaviours that generate trust

✓ Looking at ways to develop our communication networks and develop stronger relationships

"If you tell the truth you do not have to remember anything."
Mark Twain

What is trustworthiness?

When people talk about trustworthiness they use words like responsible, honest, reliable, accountable, ethical and integrity, and these are fundamental elements of becoming more influential. In many ways, trustworthiness is similar to some of the areas discussed in the previous section on credibility.

However, there is a key difference between the two. Credibility may be gained in a particular area of expertise whereas trusting someone means having confidence in them as a person. An essential characteristic of trust is its reciprocal nature – you only get it if you give it. It can take a long time to build trust, yet it can be destroyed very quickly.

"Trust is like a vase once it is broken, though you can fix it, the vase will never be the same again."

We are far more likely to listen and give consideration to the views of people that we trust than people that we don't. This means that we are more open to being influenced by someone that we trust. Have you ever questioned or challenged someone's viewpoint not because of the quality of the idea, but because of a distrust of the person delivering it?

Authenticity

"No one man can, for any considerable time, wear one face to himself and another to the multitude without finally getting bewildered as to the true one." Hawthorne

We trust people who behave authentically – authenticity happens when we match our ideas and values to the behaviours we exhibit. This is often described as being the same on the outside as on the inside. The following shows how a lack of authenticity did reduce one manager's ability to influence.

Case Study

Many years ago I worked for a manager who told me during my induction that he had an "open door policy". He explained the importance he placed on developing strong working relationships with his staff and that he valued openness and honesty. I was very encouraged by this and was looking forward to working with him and learning from him. However, as the months progressed I realised that the reality was his door was never open. If I passed him in the corridor he always said hello but did not stop walking. Difficult messages were always sent to me by email. Meetings were arranged and then cancelled, often at short notice. If I needed help or advice it was almost impossible to get. The behaviour he exhibited was totally at odds with the things that he had said. In the end, I stopped trying to consult with him and began to find ways to work round him – this resulted in distrust on both sides. The relationship quickly deteriorated and I left the department a year later.

This case study demonstrates how important authenticity is in generating trust. It is why self-awareness is such an important part of becoming more influential – we cannot behave authentically without first understanding who we are and what we believe in.

This means being clear about what our values are and using them as the basis of our decision making.

What are values?

The dictionary definition is that values are a collection of guiding, usually positive principles which one deems to be correct and desirable in life, especially regarding personal conduct.

Examples of values may include things like:

➢ Caring

➢ Enthusiasm

➢ Compassion

➢ Optimism

➢ Honesty

➢ Family

➢ Success

➢ Health

Many of us will state that something is really important to us. However, that does not actually translate into practice.

Case Study

During a course on life/work balance, one of the delegates realised that she had fallen into that trap. Although she would happily state that one of the things she valued the most was her family, the reality was that she was not demonstrating that. She told us that she was spending a lot of time working and even when she was at home she knew that her attention and focus were often elsewhere. She decided that she needed to address that in a very practical way. She began to finish work at a certain time and not check emails during the evening. She did not turn the TV on every evening so that she could have more social interaction with the family and she arranged to go out to dinner once a month with her husband.

The influential people that we have observed know their values and keep them at the front of their mind constantly. They will also talk about what they value in a way that helps others to understand their position.

Exercise: Defining your values

Make a list of the 10 values which you feel are most important to you. My top ten values are:

1 ....
2 ....
3 ....
4 ....
5 ....
6 ....
7 ....
8 ....
9 ....
10 ....

Example:
This example was written by a manager attending a course on leadership:

Value: Personal Development

What personal development means to me
Development has always been both a value and a passion for me. I have always sought out opportunities to learn new things, take up new challenges and use the value I place on learning as a foundation for both my personal and professional development. Learning also excites and inspires me and is a source of energy.

How much I connect with it in my daily life
As a leader, I have always shared this value with my team and colleagues and constantly encourage them to take up development opportunities. This was all well and good, but around 6 months ago I realised that over the last 12-18 months I had participated in no new learning experiences. I had read no new books, attended no courses or conferences, done no new research or led no new projects. I had been a learning-free zone!

I realised that the demands of both work and home had been such that very subtly I had lost touch with one of the most important values in my life and work. Both from a personal point of view and as a role model to my staff, I felt this was really unacceptable.

Having made the realisation, the first thing I did was sit down and look at what type of development I felt I needed at this stage and came up with 2 areas :

Refreshing my leadership development:
I wanted to see what new things were out there for leaders and access some form of leadership development which was group-based in the next 6 months.

Reading material:
I love books and at one of the last conferences I did attend I heard Deepak Chopra speak and was inspired by some of the concepts he was looking at – I decided to order two of his books as a starting point for getting back into reading.

Now having read this example, have a go with just 2 of your values. Identify the two values which you hold most dear and (on the next page) under each one write a paragraph about what this value means to you and how much you feel you connect with it in your daily life.

What the value .... means to me is:

How much I connect with it in my daily life is:

Two actions I will take in connection with this value are:

What the value .... means to me is:

How much I connect with it in my daily life is:

Two actions I will take in connection with this value are:

Case Study

A delegate on one of our training programmes used this exercise on her values in the following way.

I realised that I had a very strong value around collaboration and working together and although I believed in these values, they had become subsumed in my working life because everyone in my team (including me) felt overworked and stretched on a daily basis. We were all so focused on our own work that we rarely lifted our heads up to check on colleagues, ask for help and share ideas. People would constantly say things like, "Just let me get to the end of the week.", "I can't think about that now, I have to get this done by lunchtime.", "Lunchtime – what's that?" We only ever talked to complain about workload or throw out slightly bitter lines like the ones above. I was just as bad as everyone else. When I came on your course and we did the exercise on values, I decided that I wanted to start working more collaboratively, sharing work and helping other people in my team. My motivation was quite simply that I was sick of being miserable at work! I hoped that if I started to model these values then other people would follow my example and we could all be a bit happier.

I decided that the following day, I would go into work and do 2 things:
- ✓ Allocate 20 minutes in the morning and 20 minutes in the afternoon in which I would do something to help a colleague. I felt that 40 minutes away from my own tasks would neither make nor break the week!
- ✓ Ask our administrator to reinstate team meetings. We used to hold these fortnightly but stopped having them because we were all too busy.

The day started well, I looked at my work and decided to allocate my first 20 minutes at 11.00am. I stopped work at 11, stood up and said pretty loudly, "I have 20 minutes to spare, can I do anything for anyone?" The shock was quite funny really, everyone just stared at me. A couple of people muttered something like, "Wish I had 20 minutes to spare – lucky you."

I was a bit intimidated but I continued to look round and said, "Seriously, can I do anything for anyone?" One colleague said rather tentatively, "Could you just copy these for me?" and held out some reports – she then said, "I mean if you are sure." I said, "I wouldn't have offered if I didn't mean it," took the reports and went and copied them.

When I came back into the office, my colleague thanked me and said, "That was good of you." I took a deep breath and said, "Well something we did yesterday made me think that if we all used a bit of our time to help each other we may find that we can make things a bit easier. I've also asked if we can have the team meetings back. I just think we've stopped working together and we should start again, at least in small ways, if we can." A few more people were listening and a couple of people said they thought I was right and they would like to get the team meetings back.

The upshot that day was that we spent around half an hour talking about how we could work a bit better together and something's started to change. I'm not saying it was all perfect at once because it wasn't but we have continued and people are very used to "the 20 minute help out" now, which is what we have called it. I really felt I influenced my team to work differently.

Once you start to connect more strongly to your values and act on them, you are behaving authentically – this generates trust and trust is a key component of influence. Trust can be enhanced if you do keep faith with your values and others can see this. If however, we state a value and then fail to "live it" this erodes trust as people see us as less than authentic and therefore, will not believe that they can trust us. So be very aware of this – it's particularly important if you lead or manage others, be sure that when you publicly declare your values, you are able to live them in your daily life and express them in your behaviour.

Intent

Another cornerstone of our trustworthiness is having good intentions. This is about genuinely being as concerned about the other person as we are about ourselves. It is about having a clear and open agenda and ensuring that our actions and decisions are motivated by mutually serving, rather than self-serving motives.

"The moment there is suspicion about a person's motives, everything they do becomes tainted." Mahatma Ghandi

What do you believe the intent is when you hear the following?

➤ "I hear what you are saying."

➤ "With all due respect, I think you will find...."

➤ "I don't want to disagree with you, I am just playing devil's advocate."

It is rare that people believe the words in these phrases – the usual reaction is that the speaker's real intent is to undermine or manipulate. As soon as that happens our ability to influence in that situation is diminished.

Behaviours that generate trust

So how does this translate into practice? What makes us trust some people and not others?

Exercise: Behaviours that generate trust

Identify 5 people that you know and write their names down

e.g. manager, colleague, relative, friend, member of staff

Try to think of some people that you do trust and some that you do not.

1 ....

2 ....

3 ....

4 ....

5 ....

Think about the people you have identified and the general patterns of behaviour that you experience from them. Now generate two lists – those behaviours that discourage trust in the people you have identified and a second list of those behaviours that encourage trust.

Behaviours that discourage trust:

....
....
....
....
....
....
....
....
....
....

Behaviours that encourage trust:

....
....
....
....
....
....
....
....
....
....

Having run this exercise many times over the years, the following are typical examples of behaviours that people identify.

Behaviours that discourage trust:

✗ Saying different things to different people
✗ Failing to keep promises
✗ Not sharing feelings
✗ Blaming others
✗ Scapegoating others
✗ Manipulation
✗ Saying one thing and doing another
✗ Talking about people behind their backs
✗ Dishonesty
✗ Hiding or not sharing information
✗ Betraying confidences
✗ Never asking for help

Behaviours that encourage trust:

✓ Being willing and able to listen without judging
✓ Making time for people
✓ Openness
✓ Sharing information willingly
✓ Doing things without expecting anything in return
✓ Showing compassion
✓ Honesty
✓ Demonstrates integrity
✓ Practising what you preach
✓ Being pleased for people when things go well for them
✓ Giving positive feedback
✓ Having the difficult conversations when they are necessary
✓ Displaying sincerity
✓ Clear communication
✓ Being clear about your expectations of others
✓ Trusting others

Review the list above and consider which you display – this may be difficult to assess yourself and you may need to seek feedback from others.

Developing your trustworthiness

All the things that have been discussed so far in this chapter rely on people knowing you well enough to trust you. A key area we can therefore work on in becoming more influential is building and developing strong relationships.

Exercise: Building relationships

Charting your network

1. Draw a picture of yourself or write your name in the middle of the following page.
2. Identify all the people in your life that you communicate with regularly and therefore sometimes need to influence – put these names on the chart.
3. Consider how strong each relationship is - if the relationship is very strong draw a thick line between you and that person. If it is non-existent do not draw a line and if it is weak draw a dotted line.

Example:

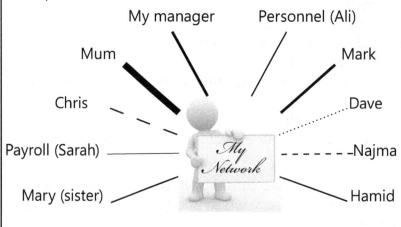

Chart your network:

Look at your network and consider the following questions:

Are there areas that need to be strengthened?

Do you invest a lot of time in some areas of your network and not enough in others?

Identify someone in your network that you feel you need to develop a more trusting relationship with.

What do you think are the reasons for the lack of trust?

Look back at the list of behaviours that generate trust and identify three things that you can do to build trust with that person.

1

2

3

Summary of Trait 3:
Trustworthiness

In summary to develop this trait, concentrate on:

✓ Being clear about what your values are and what they mean

✓ Ensuring that you are being consistent with those values and therefore behaving authentically

✓ Checking that when you are dealing with people that you are open and honest and that your intent is good. In other words, you are genuinely concerned about the other person as well as yourself

✓ Exhibiting the behaviours in your everyday life that generate trust and avoiding the ones that discourage it

✓ Investing time and energy in building relationships with people

Further Reading:

Liberating the Corporate Soul, Richard Barrett, Butterworth-Heineman, 978-0750670715

The Speed of Trust (The One Thing That Changes Everything), Stephen R Covey and Rebecca Merrill, Simon and Schuster, 978-0743295604

The Five Dysfunctions of Teams Patrick Lencioni, Jossey Bass, 978-07879-6075-9

http://www.forbes.com/sites/margiewarrell/2015/08/31/how-to-build-high-trust-relationships/#7c041857b2d0

Trait 4:
Empathy

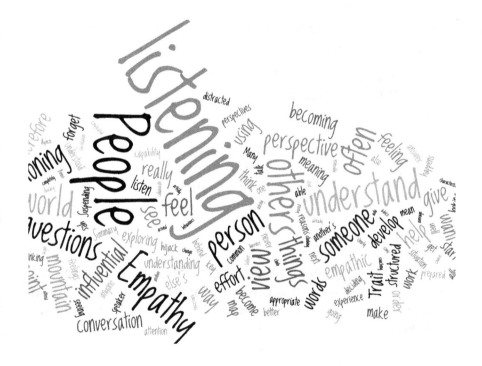

"If you learn just a single trick, Scout,
you'll get along a lot better with all kinds of folks.
You never really understand a person until
you consider things from his point of view ...
until you climb inside of his skin and walk around in it."
Atticus Finch

Trait 4:
Empathy

In this section, we will be:

✓ Defining empathy

✓ Explaining the importance of exploring other people's points of view

✓ Discussing the key skills of empathising, i.e. insightful questioning and active listening

✓ Providing guidance on how to develop your ability to empathise

"People will forget what you said, people will forget what you did, but people will never forget how you made them feel."
Bonnie Jean Wasmund

What is empathy?

Empathy is the capability to share and understand another's emotions and feelings. It is often characterised as the ability to "put oneself into another's shoes," or in some way experience what the other person is feeling.

So how does experiencing what another person is feeling help us become more influential?

If someone makes us feel:

➢ Understood

➢ Listened to

➢ Respected

➢ Intelligent

➢ Appreciated

➢ Valued or

➢ Trusted

then we will want to reciprocate and will therefore become open to helping them feel the same way.

People who we feel understand us are the people we are open to being influenced by. There is often a myth that empathic people are from the "soft and fluffy" school of thought. Nothing could be further from the truth. Empathic people succeed in life BECAUSE they can influence and collaborate successfully with other people.

When people talk about becoming more influential they often think about impressing their point on others. Influential people understand that to influence anyone they have to be able to understand their view of the world. They get the other point of view and work with what others think, feel and believe.

Maps of the world – exploring other points of view

Consider the above image. We often sit on top of our own mountain and focus only on the view from there. This is the view which is often described as our map of the world and is formulated from our own perspective and experience. In order to influence we have to be prepared to climb down our own mountain and get to the top of someone else's mountain to see the world from their perspective.

I love this metaphor because in addition to making the point about seeing the world differently, it also implies a sense of effort. Empathy and really understanding others does take effort. Naturally, we can see our own perspective easily, to put that perspective aside in order to truly consider someone else's is quite a stretch. However, the bottom line is that we will never become influential without being prepared to do this.

When people ask for better communication they are asking for better understanding, so when we are able to make others feel understood – we really do start to implant a feeling which stays with others for a long time and will inevitably increase our influence with them.

Many people come to training and coaching sessions wanting to change a perspective in someone else. Nine times out of ten, they will only be looking at the situation from their own map of the world. There is a good case study about other points of view using the six steps at the end of the book.

The skills of empathising – insightful questioning and active listening

The key skills we use when exploring someone else's map of the world are insightful questioning and active listening. These are also clearly skills of a strong communication capability which is discussed in Trait 6. However, because they are core to empathy we felt it was appropriate to cover them in this chapter.

Insightful questioning

What do we mean by insightful questioning?

The kind of questions that create dialogue and help to draw people out so that you can really understand their point of view are the kind of questions we are talking about here.

These are primarily open questions, those which open up a conversation by prompting a more detailed answer rather than those which just invite a yes or no response. They are used to prompt both yourself and the other person to deeper insights.

Open questions allow the speaker to help you understand their viewpoint. Closed questions can only give you information. A closed question has a right or wrong (and often short) answer. E.g. How many reams of paper are left? Where is the report? Did you find the room?

Some useful open questions to help foster empathic conversations are:

➢ "Tell me more about................"

➢ "Can you give me an example?"

➢ "I hadn't thought of it in that way. Please could you give me more detail?"

➢ "Can you help me to understand your viewpoint?"

➢ "How is that affecting you?"

➢ "What do you want to happen?"

➢ "How would you like to see this develop from here?"

➢ "What stops you from.............. ?"

➢ "What are the results you want?"

➢ "What outcome would you choose?"

➢ "What are your thoughts about .... ?"

➢ "How can I support you with this?"

Active listening

What do we mean by active listening?

Active listening is an intent to listen for meaning as well as for words. This means paying attention to the feeling behind the words and expressing understanding of the meaning the person wants to convey.

Exercise: Barriers to listening

Think about the last time you were trying to listen to someone and you found it difficult – what were the main reasons that you struggled to listen properly?

....

....

....

....

Some common reasons for switching off are:

✗ Being biased about either the person or the topic and therefore deciding that it is not worth listening.

✗ Formulating our own argument. This is such a common mistake when we passionately want to influence a situation. We are listening only for cues that will allow us to jump in with our next point.

✗ Becoming distracted by other things that are going on around us.

✗ Becoming distracted by things that we are thinking.

✗ Drifting off because what we are hearing is too complicated or complex.

✗ Deciding that we already know what someone is going to say and therefore there is no need to listen.

You may have listed other reasons and it is important to recognise how hard it is to listen well – our average listening span is about 7 minutes and so it is something that we do have to work at.

Think about the barriers that you identified in that exercise and decide to consciously start to practise stopping yourself doing those things in your next conversation.

Influential people work very hard at both their questioning and listening skills, and using these skills artfully is one of the most respectful and empathic things you can do for anyone.

Active listening is completely different in its quality from autopilot listening. It is a structured way of listening and responding to others – it focuses attention on the speaker. If we do not make a conscious effort to do this, we often hijack the conversation very quickly. Usually this hijack occurs within the first minute of a conversation and happens when we start to talk about our own experiences or begin to give advice. Suspending our judgement in order to fully attend to the other person immediately increases our ability to understand and therefore influence.

Aspects of active listening include:

✓ Looking at the person and suspending other things you are doing and thinking about.

✓ Listening not merely to the words, but the feelings behind the words.

✓ Becoming aware of the things which can stop you listening – we can all switch off for various reasons and it is important to recognise that whenever this happens you are not really listening.

✓ Using verbal reinforcers such as "I see" and "yes" when appropriate.

✓ Avoiding distracting behaviours such as fidgeting.

✓ Seeking clarification if the meaning is not clear.

✓ Minimising interruptions.

Developing your empathy

The following couple of exercises give you a structured approach to seeing others' perspectives.

Exercise: Image exchange

Think of a person or group that you have difficulty empathising with. This exercise is a useful way to try and understand the other person's point of view. Write down your side of the story and then try and think what the other person's side of the story might be

My side of the story is:

....

....

....

I think ....'s side of the story is:

....

....

....

What might you need to do to empathise with them more?

....

....

....

Exercise: Alternative viewpoints

This exercise can be used on your own or with a team when trying to look at an issue from a number of different viewpoints. Place the issue in the centre of a piece of paper. Write all the names of people or groups who may have a view about that issue around the outside. Work round the stakeholders offering ideas about what you think that person's or groups' perspective on the issue would be.

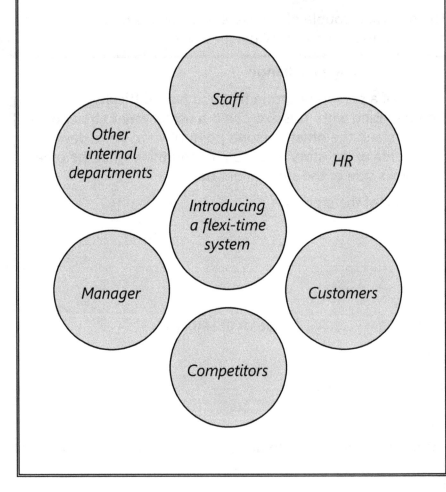

Draw your own diagram about an issue that is relevant to you.

List 5 ideas someone else might think about the issue:

1 ....

2 ....

3 ....

4 ....

5 ....

Summary of trait 4:
Empathy

In summary, to develop this trait concentrate on:

✓ Getting off your own mountain and climbing up the other mountain! Make the effort!

✓ Using insightful questions and active listening

✓ Develop your ability to see others' perspectives by using structured exercises

Further Reading:

The Seven Habits of Highly Effective People, Stephen R Covey, Simon and Schuster, 978-0684858395

NLP at Work, Sue Knight, Nicholas Brealey, 978-1857883022

Social Intelligence, Daniel Goleman, Arrow Books, 978-0099464921

www.danielgoleman.info

www.businessballs.com/empathy.htm

Trait: 5
Inspirational

"There are those who look at things the
way they are, and ask why ...
I dream of things that never were,
and ask why not?"

Robert Francis Kennedy

Trait 5: Inspirational

In this section we will be:

✓ Clarifying why the ability to inspire is part of influencing

✓ Defining what being inspirational really means

✓ Developing your ability to inspire yourself and tap into your power to inspire

✓ Providing guidance on how to develop the skill of enthusing and inspiring others

"Remember if you want to become an inspiration to others, you must first become an inspiration to yourself." Gareth Brown.

What do we mean by inspirational?

The next trait which influential people demonstrate is that of inspiration.

Few people would question how important the ability to inspire is to influencing, and yet many people will flinch at the idea of inspiring others. We turn away from our own ability to do that, thinking that the ability to inspire is granted only to a few – those special charismatic ones in the world.

Yet, when we ask people who has inspired them, most people speak of someone they know, often a parent, a teacher, sometimes someone they have worked with or for. This indicates that we all have the power to inspire.

It is crucial to your influencing power that you believe that you hold the power to inspire others. As we unpick inspiration, keep that thought in the forefront of your mind.

So, what is inspiration? The dictionary definitions are:

"Arousal of the mind to special or unusual activity or creativity;
a product of your creative thinking and work;
a sudden intuition as part of solving a problem or
stirring to a particular emotion or action."

Inspiration therefore, is what moves us, what stimulates us, what creates our capacity for action. We believe that this is a particularly useful way of thinking about inspiration and if you consider those definitions, most of us will be able to fairly easily identify occasions when we have inspired ourselves.

We have perhaps been inspired when:

✓ We have produced something out of our own creative thinking.

✓ Had moments when we felt stimulated by an exciting idea to special or unusual activity or creativity.

✓ Had a flash of insight which helped us to solve a problem or felt stirred into action.

These moments are the first steps to becoming an inspiration to ourselves.

Inspiring yourself

Influential people not only make the most of such moments but they work at creating more inspiration within their own lives and thereby inspire others to do the same. Influential people inspire in us not just a belief in them but in ourselves.

> *"If your actions inspire others to dream more, learn more,*
> *do more and become more, you are a leader."*
> *John Quincy Adams*

Influential people also radiate enthusiasm. If you feel inspired yourself, then it is easier to feel and project enthusiasm. However, influential people can be roused to enthusiasm simply by another's great idea. We often hear people say that they sometimes lose touch with their own inspiration and don't feel they are inspired "enough", but they can still feel enthused to encourage someone else's idea and therefore, start to feel more inspired themselves. Whether your inspiration comes from creating inspiring moments for yourself or by inspiring others – it still taps into your creativity and strengthens your influencing capacity.

The key is to recognise how you become inspired.

WE ALL HAVE THE POWER TO INSPIRE

Elements of being inspirational are:

✓ Inspiring and motivating yourself

✓ Creating inspired action

✓ Encouraging others to get inspired

84

As we connect with our ability to inspire, we express qualities of enthusiasm, excitement and confidence. We are able then to pass this onto others because we believe it. Action is also a part of this - taking action in itself is inspirational. Influential people act. They do not allow their fears to hold them back, they move forward and do something rather than nothing.

The following exercises are designed to help you increase your ability to inspire and motivate yourself, create inspired action and encourage others to get inspired.

Exercise: Inspirational moments and inspirational action

This exercise is designed to help you think through your own inspirational moments and what actions you are creating as a result.

Consider those dictionary definitions again:-

"Arousal of the mind to special or unusual activity or creativity;
a product of your creative thinking and work;
a sudden intuition as part of solving a problem or
stirring to a particular emotion or action."

Identify any occasions in the last 6 months when you have been stimulated by an exciting idea or thought that

➤ boosted your activity or creativity
➤ produced something creative
➤ gave you an intuition, sudden idea or change of perspective which has helped you solve a problem
➤ emotionally stirred you into action

Please list any occasions which fall into these categories on the following page. If at this stage, the list is quite short or even if you cannot think of anything, don't worry, the purpose of this is to simply identify if inspiration is a trait that you need to work on.

My inspirational moments in the last 6 months:

....

....

....

....

....

....

....

When you have completed your list, think about:

How easy was it to think of inspirational moments?

How many occasions did you identify? There is no rule about how many inspired thoughts and actions you can and should have, this is a simple check for you to decide if you are accessing your inspiration as much as you could.

What action followed on from your first inspiration?

What other ideas have been stimulated by this exercise?

....

....

....

....

....

....

....

....

One of the great things about thinking about inspiration is..... you get more inspired!

Tips to increase your inspirational moments:

Think about your previous list. When you were creating inspired ideas and inspired actions :

➢ Were you alone or was someone with you?

➢ If there was someone with you, who was it and what was their contribution to your moment of inspiration?

➢ Where were you?

➢ Was there anything you were seeing, hearing, touching, smelling or tasting which contributed to your moment of inspiration?

➢ What was your state of mind at the time?

➢ How were you feeling physically?

➢ Did you do something specific to help your creativity? If so, what was it?

The purpose of this reflection is to start your thinking process on how your moments of inspiration are created. Many people find that a particular place, person, view, smell, piece of music, poem, etc. helps them to feel inspired, and to create more inspiration in your life, you create circumstances which will assist that process.

Example:

These are some of things that inspire me:
- ✓ Conversations with people who energise me
- ✓ My vision board
- ✓ The Secret by Rhonda Byrne
- ✓ Reading books and accessing talks and webinars from amazing teachers and mentors: Tony Robbins, Bernadette Doyle, Brene Brown, James Lavers, and many, many more
- ✓ Songs, e.g. The Breath You Take, Bridge Over Troubled Water, The Whole of the Moon
- ✓ Stories of people doing the seemingly impossible, e.g. all our Paralympian heroes and heroines
- ✓ Water, the ocean, rivers, lakes and walking in nature
- ✓ Swimming
- ✓ Inspirational quotes, e.g. Go confidently in the direction of your dreams, live the life you have imagined
- ✓ Poetry, particularly the poem "The Journey" by Mary Oliver

If you can identify those things which help you feel inspired, you can develop ways of accessing them when you need inspiration.

Some suggestions for staying close to your inspiration are:
- ✓ Create a visualisation board with pictures which inspire
- ✓ Keep quotations somewhere visible
- ✓ Sign up to a motivational website
- ✓ Keep downloads or CDs which inspire you accessible where you can play them easily and listen to them often
- ✓ Buy inspirational books
- ✓ Practise meditating on the things which inspire you

If you stay connected to those things which inspire you, you will feel more energised and creative and this energy will help you to grow your ability to inspire others.

Exercise: Things that inspire me

List 3 things that inspire you:

1
2
3

Inspiring others

"Life doesn't require that we be the best, only that we try our best." H.Jackson Brown

You may think – what about those days when I feel as if my inspiration has gone, can I still be inspirational to others? Yes you can, because when it comes to inspiring others, one thing stands out – enthusiasm! When we are enthusiastic and optimistic about someone's talents, ideas or qualities, we strike a chord which starts to help others to feel inspired. It is a lot easier, as we said before, to radiate enthusiasm when you feel inspired, but not impossible. Many people will know that even on a low day when your child, partner or colleague needs some active encouragement, you find it and by starting to express enthusiasm for their ideas, you automatically start to perk up and feel more inspired yourself.

Enthusing and inspiring others will always increase your energy and sense of inspiration. This is a virtuous circle and it doesn't matter whether on a particular day you start from feeling inspired yourself or by getting energised and enthused by someone else's idea, it all increases your ability to become inspired and to inspire others. Enthusiasm is contagious in the most positive way.

One of the results of this contagion is that you will become someone who actively encourages ideas from other people, and being an idea grower is one of the most powerful characteristics of influential people. An influential person is rarely precious about their own ideas, they will fully acknowledge how inspirational they find the ideas of others, and will openly express enthusiasm, praise and encouragement to others to both have ideas and to act on them. Thus, influential people help to grow inspiration in other people.

One of the enemies of inspiration is our inner critic which we refer to in the section on knowing what you want and believing you can achieve it (trait 1). Influential people increase their ability to inspire by both managing their own inner critic and helping others to manage their inner critic. One of the greatest deterrents to creativity is the inner voice that constantly whispers in our ear that we're not good enough, that nobody will approve of what we're doing and that they don't really like us anyway. No one other than yourself can do the work of eradicating the inner critic completely. However, it is possible to help others listen to their positive voice rather than their negative voice and therefore, help them to increase their creativity and inspiration. This is where influential people score – they help other people manage that inner critic and keep it in the right place.

Another powerful way to encourage others to become inspired is to stimulate their imagination and create situations and environments in which ideas can flourish. Pixar is a company known for innovation and creativity. Films such as Toy Story, The Incredibles and Finding Nemo have demonstrated that, and yet, unlike many other film studios, all their stories, worlds and characters are created internally. Part of their ability to do this comes from consistently applying three operating principles:

✓ Everyone in the organisation must have freedom to communicate with anyone.

✓ It must be safe for everyone to offer ideas.

✓ We must stay close to innovations that are happening in the academic community.

Tips for inspiring other people:

➢ Ask them what enthuses them and encourage them to talk about those things.

➢ Radiate enthusiasm.

➢ Praise people for new ideas and encourage them to develop their ideas further.

➢ Get comfortable with ambiguity.

➢ Encourage curiosity and questions, actively praise people for being curious.

➢ Use creative techniques such as imagery, metaphor or storytelling and encourage others to do the same.

➢ Provide opportunities for people to work in inspiring environments. Think about space, light, pictures, music, colour, nature and bring them into your environment if possible.

➢ Allow ideas to incubate and reach maturity (both your own ideas and those of others).

Some of the above suggestions such as creative imagery may feel unfamiliar. However, they can be woven into all kinds of situations if you allow yourself some space to think slightly differently. The following example demonstrates this.

Case Study

We did this exercise in a workshop, in which one of the delegates wanted to find an inspirational image to use as part of a presentation to a group of her staff to explain how the service they were providing in the university was changing and would need to adapt to accommodate a wider cross-section of students.

She came up with the idea of using a tea towel she had bought with a map of the London Underground on it. She started to describe how routes through the university were going to be like a train service. Traditionally, students had got on the train at the start of a journey and stayed on it until the end. However, there were now many more choices. Firstly, people can choose which route they want to take (the qualification) and they can choose how long the journey is going to be (full time study, part time, distance learning etc.). People can get off the train and break their journey for a few days or a year. The lines and routes on the map intersect and cross over, which allows people to change course or direction fairly easily if they want to. As she continued with the analogy, people became quite animated and started to describe ways that the service they offered would need to change to meet the changing environment. Her feedback was that the session went exceptionally well and the image prompted all kinds of ideas that no one had expressed before and really motivated the whole team.

This is a great example of how an influential person can use an inspirational image to encourage inspiration in others.

Exercise: The power of story telling

Stories attach emotions to things that happen and therefore are more memorable and inspiring than facts and figures.

Identify an individual or group that you would like to encourage to generate more ideas of actions.

Think about an occasion when you, someone else, or a team have needed to come up with new ideas.

Identify the obstacles they faced.

What did they do to overcome them?

What was the happy ending?

Develop a 5 minute story:

Summary of trait 5: Inspirational

In summary, to develop this trait concentrate on:

✓ Believing in your power to inspire

✓ Focusing on your inspirational moments

✓ Making time to connect with people and things which inspire you

✓ Being enthusiastic about other people's ideas, talents and qualities

✓ Encouraging curiosity in yourself and others

✓ Praising others and actively asking for their ideas

✓ Capturing ideas which inspire, do not let them drift away

✓ Practising developing creative images

✓ Acting on your inspiration!

Further Reading:

Thinkertoys - A Handbook of Business Creativity, Michael Michalko, Ten Speed Press, 978-1580087735
Boost Your Creative Intelligence, Harry Alder, Kogan Page, 978-0749437060
Creative Manager's Pocketbook, John Townsend and Jacques Favier, Management Pocketbooks, 978-1870471695
The Eighth Habit, Stephen R Covey, 978-0743206839
The Storytelling Animal, How Stories Make Us Human, Jonathan Gottschall, Mariner, 9780544002340
Contagious: Why Things Catch On, Jonah Berger, 9781451686586
www.positive-way.com   www.stephencovey.com

Trait 6:
Strong communication capability

"I am the most spontaneous speaker in the world
because every word, every gesture,
and every retort has been carefully rehearsed."

George Bernard Shaw

Trait 6: Strong communication capability

In this section we will be:

✓ Defining strong communication capability

✓ Clarifying the elements of a strong communication capability

> ➤ Verbal impact

>> ‣ The ability to structure verbal communication with clarity and logic
>> ‣ Contextualising your language
>> ‣ Avoiding unhelpful language patterns
>> ‣ Ability to structure insightful questions and listen really well

> ➤ Non-verbal impact

>> ‣ Voice projection and great use of emphasis and tone
>> ‣ Image and personal presentation
>> ‣ Congruence

✓ Written impact

✓ Impact in presentations

"Good communication is as stimulating as black coffee, and just as hard to sleep after."
Anne Morrow Lindbergh

What is a strong communication capability?

"The ability to communicate powerfully in a range of ways and in a range of situations."

Influential people are at ease with all the elements of a strong communication capability, and are able to express themselves using a variety of those elements as appropriate. This trait is the catalyst for using the other traits. We must be able to communicate our sense of purpose, our empathy, our expertise, our open-mindedness to others in order to influence them. Honing our communication capability is vital to increasing our influence.

As well as being skilled in all the elements of a strong communication capability, influential people are able to judge which method of communication is appropriate to particular situations. This is very important, as a powerful message can be killed by the wrong method of communication and is immeasurably strengthened by the right method.

Daniel Goleman, author of Emotional Intelligence, speaks of rich and lean or thick and thin communication. Face to face conversation is rich communication, email is lean communication.

Misunderstandings are highly prevalent in lean communication. Influential people choose rich over lean communication whenever possible as you are always better able to influence if you are in a rich communication environment.

The elements of a strong communication capability

We have identified 4 main elements of a strong communication capability that are important for influential people to master:

1. Verbal impact
2. Non-verbal impact
3. Written impact
4. Impact in formal presentations

There are different aspects of these 4 main elements which we have also looked at within this section to help clarify how to develop your communication capability to its best effect.

Exercise:
What are your strengths in communicating with others?

Think of 3 of your most recent successful communications. What made them work?

Verbal impact

Verbal impact includes a number of different aspects:

- ✓ Structuring our verbal communication with clarity and logic
- ✓ Contextualising our language for the situation
- ✓ Avoiding unhelpful language patterns
- ✓ Ability to structure insightful questions and listen exceptionally well

Exercise: Listen to the world's best speakers

There are a lot of famous speakers who, by the power of how they spoke and what they said, changed history.

Have a listen to the following with your eyes closed:

I have a dream, Martin Luther King

Britain's finest hour, Winston Churchill

One World, Mahatma Gandhi

Ability to structure our verbal communication with clarity and logic.

Many people lose their power to influence because of an inability to structure their conversations. It is really important to check on the logic and flow of your verbal communication. Waffling and rambling are not traits of influential people.

One of the reasons that logic and flow can get lost in verbal communication is that few people actually plan important conversations. We tend to plan written conversation in a much more structured way than we do verbal. Influential people plan their important verbal communication in as much detail as they do their written. Many situations in which you need to influence hang on a particular conversation, be it one on one or in a group or meeting situation. These conversations need to be planned carefully if you are to make them as influential/ effective as possible.

If this is an important conversation and you want it to be an influential conversation, it deserves time and effort in preparation. Influential people prepare for important conversations!

Planning important conversations does not mean that you have to lose all spontaneity. There is real joy and power in those conversations that start at one point and then range into unexpected areas, resulting in great ideas and new thinking. Some people believe that if they start to plan for the important conversations in their life then they will lose that spontaneity and willingness to allow new thinking to emerge. This is not so. Our experience shows that paradoxically, a plan gives you the confidence and ability to open yourself to new thinking and new ideas because you have a focus which decreases your anxiety. You know that wherever the conversation goes, you can bring it back if you need to and allow it to develop further if you want to. Structure and planning are not the enemy of spontaneity.

100

Tips to help you structure your verbal communication:

When planning an important conversation or delivering an important message, think about the following:

✓ What do I hope this conversation will achieve?

✓ What might the other person/people be thinking about the situation?

✓ What is their map of the world?

✓ What might they want to achieve?

✓ What are my concerns?

✓ What may their concerns be?

✓ How could we manage our mutual concerns?

✓ Am I making any assumptions? If so what are they?

✓ What is the checklist of things we need to discuss?

✓ What is the right time and place to have this conversation?

✓ Write a plan which covers all the above points. This is not in order to read from a script but to clarify your thinking beforehand. Reading from a script or plan would lessen your ability to influence rather than increase it.

✓ Rehearse with someone you trust who can give you feedback or at least rehearse out loud by yourself. Speaking aloud is very different from running something through in your mind. You will "hear" different things.

✓ Review your plan after practise and change it if need be.

✓ Practise again!

✓ Make sure that you practise enough so that your plan is firmly in your mind as you enter the conversation.

Contextualising your language

A second element of powerful verbal communication is the ability to use language which is appropriate to the context. Influential people understand the importance of contextualising their language to the situation and the person or people they are trying to influence.

There are a number of aspects to consider when choosing the right kind of language to use. For instance, if you want to inspire as part of your influencing, then you need to choose language which is impactful and rich. Many highly influential figures are skilled in the use of rich language, creative imagery, metaphor and storytelling.

Consider Martin Luther King's "I have a dream" speech. His words have been repeated and replayed time and time again, and their power is still as fresh and inspirational today as when he first gave the speech. Think of the following phrase:

"Now is the time to lift our nation from the quicksands of racial injustice to the solid rock of brotherhood." Martin Luther King

The picture painted and the feelings that it evokes capture the imagination. In that context, a factual account of racial injustice would not have been nearly as influential.

If, however, you are facing a group of engineers who you wish to influence to use a particular piece of equipment or work a particular site, creative imagery is unlikely to be as impactful and may indeed be seen as fanciful or trite. Factual language, clarity and plain English will serve you much better.

Influencing a group of youths in a deprived area of an inner city to take part in a community activity may require you to use informal language in order to have a conversation which they will find meaningful. Formal business language would be useless.

Influential people understand the concept of contextualising their language, to the situation in order to increase their influence.

Many people are only at ease using a particular form of language and within many organisations today business speak or management speak both obscures meaning and dumbs down the vocabulary. Influential people can say what they mean, have a wide vocabulary, and tailor their language to the context.

Tips to help you develop the ability to contextualise your language:

✓ Widen your vocabulary by consciously using tools such as a Thesaurus and practising using different words to express your meaning.

✓ Study plain English and avoid jargon and over-complicated language.

✓ Practise thinking of and describing imaginative images with exercises such as the one in the chapter on inspiration.

✓ Write down a list of metaphors which appeal to you and start to include these in your conversations when appropriate.

✓ Familiarise yourself with the type of language used by various groups and individuals. Practise using a range of language styles in different contexts.

Avoiding unhelpful language patterns

Following on from the topic of contextualising your language, it is also worth looking at any language patterns you habitually use. We develop not just our vocabulary over time but also our patterns of language and there are several language patterns that should be avoided or at least used sparingly, particularly when we are trying to influence others.

These include:

- ✗ **The exaggerated** – words such as always, never, everybody, and all often limit the scope for conversation – only use these when it is true!

- ✗ **The forcing** – telling people that they must, should or ought to do something usually produces a defensive or antagonistic response.

- ✗ **The definitive** – this language pattern involves making opinions sound like facts. It is the fine distinction between, "This is the only way to do the job," and, "I believe this is the right way to do the job." The first statement discourages discussion where the second one leaves the door open for debate.

- ✗ **Deletions** – these are examples of language where parts of the meaning have been omitted. This is where "they" come into their own. As in, "They wouldn't let us do that here". This language pattern implies that the speaker has no influence over what is happening around them.

- ✗ **Clichés** – these are expressions or phrases that have become trite through overuse. Clichés can sound both boring and patronising if we are not careful. (Think of Ricky Gervais in the TV series The Office!) They are thought of as clichéd because they have been overused, so can also give the impression of lazy thinking. They are best avoided.

Tips to avoid unhelpful language patterns:

✓ Become aware of your language patterns and check yourself to see if you are using or overusing any of the above. Although it makes many people cringe initially, having a tape or video of yourself is incredibly helpful to study both your voice and your language patterns. Many voice coaches will offer this service.

✓ Get feedback if possible. A discussion on unhelpful language patterns with a trusted group of colleagues and friends can generate helpful feedback on any patterns you may be unaware of.

Ability to structure insightful questions and to listen really well

We have already dealt with skilful questioning and active listening in the chapter on empathy. However, it is such an important part of strong communication capability that it is worth reinforcing again.

Our verbal impact is not just about our ability to deliver our own messages. The way we question and listen to others is a very large part of the impact of our verbal communication. Insightful questioning is highly influential. David Taylor, the author of The Naked Leader, talks of a meeting about a new project in which all he did was repeat over and over again, "How does this discussion move us forward?" He says that people still talk of his contribution to the success of that project although it was several years ago.

Listening really well to someone is also highly influential. As we spoke about in the chapter on empathy, someone who listens to us and makes us feel understood is someone we will be prepared to listen to in return. Influential people understand the power of skilful questions and are excellent listeners.

Tips to increase your questioning and listening ability

✓ Seek out exercises on questioning and listening. There are lots which can be accessed on the internet by searching for communication skills or questioning and listening. We have provided a couple in the chapter on empathy.

✓ Write a list of useful questions which you could use in a variety of situations. Just writing the list will help to embed these in your mind.

✓ Always be aware of when you are listening and when you are not listening. Make a conscious effort to bring yourself back whenever you switch off.

Non-verbal impact

Much has been written about non-verbal impact and its importance to how we are perceived. Impressions are based upon instinct and emotion, not on rational thought or in-depth investigation. They are the products of the associations we make between outward characteristics and the inner qualities we believe they reflect. Many of these outward characteristics are non-verbal.

Therefore, to increase your influence it is vital that you pay as much attention to your non-verbal impact as to that of your verbal impact. We are going to look at several areas of non-verbal impact which we believe are key to honing your communication capability.

These include:

✓ Voice projection

✓ Use of emphasis and tone

✓ Image and personal presentation

✓ Congruence

Voice projection and great use of emphasis and tone

Influential people are aware of the quality of their voice. It sounds obvious, but volume and projection of voice have a big impact on how influential we can be.

Flat tones and lack of emphasis are blocks to people receiving the impact of what we have to say. Training the voice is not just for professional presenters and singers. Often we can correct problems such as speaking too quietly, varying our tone, speaking too quickly and use of emphasis ourselves once we are aware of them. As mentioned earlier, getting yourself taped or videoed in order to listen to how your voice sounds to others is a really useful thing to do, in order to become aware of any problems. Voice coaching is another option to help you make the most of your voice. In fact, many influential people in public life do get help with their voice.

Understanding the power of your voice and taking measures to maximise it to best effect can strongly increase your communication capability.

Tips to maximise the power of your voice:

✓ Get a tape or video of yourself in order to become aware of how your voice sounds to others.

✓ Decide on anything you need to correct and practise speaking more slowly, varying your tones, etc.

✓ Get feedback from others on how you sound.

✓ Think about accessing voice coaching.

Image and personal presentation

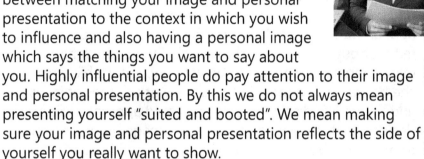

Image is a controversial topic, but in our opinion it does matter! The key is the balance between matching your image and personal presentation to the context in which you wish to influence and also having a personal image which says the things you want to say about you. Highly influential people do pay attention to their image and personal presentation. By this we do not always mean presenting yourself "suited and booted". We mean making sure your image and personal presentation reflects the side of yourself you really want to show.

It has long been asserted that we make up our minds about people we meet for the first time within two minutes – indeed some research shows that it takes as little as thirty seconds, and some of the latest thinking puts it at two seconds!

Although the jury is still out on the exact length of time, whether you take the maximum two minutes or the minimum two seconds, what this very clearly shows is that we make extremely swift decisions about people when we meet them for the first time. Most of us are aware of this on a subconscious if not a conscious level, and are also open to changing our minds if and when we get to know people better. How many times have you said or had said to you, "You are nothing like I thought you were when we first met."

Preparing ourselves in terms of the personal impact we will make in those first vital minutes can set the tone of any relationship and give you the opportunity to build from the right place.

Case Study

Working with a group on personal presentation, one member of the group was a children and young peoples' worker and was involved in involving children in outdoor and leisure activities. She was concerned because she had been invited to speak at a conference and wanted to appear authentic, yet have credibility with the audience. She felt that buying a suit for the occasion would be entirely inappropriate, as she would be very uncomfortable – yet she hesitated to appear in her usual work clothes of jeans and t-shirt. We discussed how she could approach this and decided that she needed to take her image up one notch to give her a boost, but not try to be something she was not. Smart trousers, blouse and boots worked for her – she felt and looked right. A business suit would have totally worked against her. Again, if she was going to speak to a community group, then jeans and t-shirt would be entirely right as it would give the image she wanted to present.

Tips to develop your image and personal presentation:

✓ Pay attention to your image – it sounds obvious but many people do not.

✓ Remember, being casual is not the same as being untidy and badly groomed.

✓ Get help if you need it – image consultancies abound or just use a friend whose sense of style you admire.

✓ Present the image you want to present – make it appropriate to the situation.

Congruence

What do we mean by congruence? It is a Latin word that means to come together, to agree. In the context we are discussing, congruence refers to our ability to deliver a congruent message, a clear single message as opposed to a mixed message. The process of giving a mixed message is sometimes referred to as "leakage" – we leak non-verbally what we are actually thinking! Incongruence is noticeable. We can see from non-verbal signals such as lack of eye contact, awkward gestures, etc., when someone is saying something that they are clearly not comfortable about. This makes other people feel uncomfortable as we do not know which bit of the message to respond to – do we accept what is being said or follow our much stronger impression that it is not meant?

Our non-verbal impact needs to match our verbal impact for our message to be perceived as congruent. Face to face communication is made up of three things:

➢ The words we use

➢ The way we say them – tone, pitch, emphasis, volume, etc.

➢ The body language we exhibit

When we are congruent, these three elements are matched. When they are saying the same thing then 99% of the impact comes from the words. However, when the words, tone and body language do not match, then only 7% of the impact comes from the words and 93% from the way they are delivered. This means that all your work on verbal impact can be ruined if your voice and the body language which make up your non-verbal impact are incongruent.

As it says in the song, "It ain't what you do, it's the way that you do it...."

Imagine the following conversations:

Person 1 asked, *"Is anything wrong?"*

Person 2 looked like this

and replied, *"Nothing,"* with a hesitant voice.

Person 1 said, *"Sorry I am late."*

Person 2 looked like this:

He said *"It's OK. We really appreciate you turning up at all."* in a voice that was heavily sarcastic with extra emphasis on the words *at all.*

In these examples do you think you would believe what was being **said**?

It is key to recognise how important this is when talking about communication capability.

We feel comfortable with people who behave congruently – we believe them and we believe their message. This inevitably leads to a stronger influencing capacity.

Tips to improve your congruence:

✓ Back to the idea of a video again! To really know how congruent your verbal and non-verbal communication is, you need to be able to see yourself. As with voice, many training providers on presentation skills or image will provide a videoing service and it is well worth investing in this.

✓ If the idea of a video is too excruciating, then try it out in front of the mirror. Practise delivering an important message and watch yourself. This is less effective than video as you do not see as much but will still help.

✓ Get feedback – you could make this part of a group or team exercise. Everyone could practise delivering important messages and getting feedback on how congruent they appeared.

✓ This really is an area where you need external input, either as feedback or use of some tool to be able to watch yourself back. Preferably both!

Written impact

Increasing your influence means increasing your written impact as well as your verbal and non-verbal impact. Many people concentrate on one aspect, but to become more influential it is very important to cover all types of communication. There are a number of aspects to written communication including: constructing reports, writing letters, email protocol, PowerPoint presentations, articles and books. The wider our range of written communication skills, the more influential we can be on paper or screen as well as in person.

It is easier to misunderstand written communication than verbal because of the issue of rich and lean communication methods referred to at the beginning of the chapter. Written communication is leaner than verbal therefore, it is easier to misinterpret. You need to consider both potential for misunderstanding and misinterpretation.

Examples of written howlers:

From letters to councils:
"Our lavatory seat is broken in half and now it is in three pieces."
"Our kitchen floor is damp. We have two children and would like a third so will you please send someone around to do something about it."

From minutes of a meeting:
"I have discussed the issue of filling the stationery cupboard with my colleagues."

From student essays:
"Control of infectious diseases is very important in case an academic breaks out."

Written howlers are funny to read but embarrassing for the person who has written them. Written communication is one of the most common ways people can damage or maximise their credibility. Make sure your written communication positively helps you increase your influence.

Tips to develop your written impact:

✓ Review your written skills and decide which ones you want to improve.

✓ Look at taking training courses – there are many correspondence and online courses covering writing skills.

✓ Develop both creative and business writing skills. Don't restrict yourself to purely business writing skills – many business reports benefit from the judicious use of imagery, metaphor and anecdotes. A language that has grown around business communications often makes them way too bland to be influential. Learn both types of writing and use both!

✓ Always proofread and get other people to check important pieces of written communication for mistakes or howlers.

Impact in presentations

Formal presentations are such a big part of business life today that we could not end communication capability without mentioning them. They play a key role in many situations in which we are trying to influence the outcome. Giving a short presentation forms part of a lot of job interviews, tendering processes and bids for funding.

Speaking in public is also a powerful way to build your reputation. Presenting draws on verbal, non-verbal and written impact so all the previous information is relevant. However, they also include specific use of technology and confidence in group situations.

Influential people develop their presenting skills usually by both taking presenting courses and by practise. The mindset of "I hate presentations" or "I can't do presentations" is not helpful. As we will discuss in flexible thinking, it is possible to change a mindset and once you do, it is one of the easiest skills to get help with, as there are lots of great courses and books specifically on presenting really well.

Tips to develop your presentation skills

✓ Review your presentations and get feedback on how influential they are.

✓ Look for a good presentation skills course – even experienced presenters benefit from a refresher and feedback.

✓ Practise presenting in safe situations, then when you faced with a really important situation it will feel easier.

✓ Effective presentations have a clear structure – a beginning, a middle and an end.

✓ Remember that the peak of concentration for most people is in the first few minutes of a presentation. It is therefore imperative that you start with something that captures the audience's attention. This could be an interesting statistic, a relevant quote, an anecdote or a story.

✓ Most presenters find the first few minutes are the most stressful part of a presentation. Ensure that you have scripted, learned and rehearsed the opening. This should include who you are, the structure of the presentation, the objectives and an attention grabber.

✓ Our average listening span is seven minutes so ensure your presentation is punctuated with visual aids and interaction.

✓ Remember to consider why the audience is there and keep relating the content of your presentation back to their needs.

✓ Don't let the presentation run out of steam at the end – have a clear summary and an impactful way to finish.

Summary of trait 6:
Strong communication capability

In summary, to develop this trait concentrate on:

✓ Your ability to be at ease with a variety of methods of communication

✓ Choosing the right method – remember rich and lean!

✓ Work with the tips on the different elements - communication is complex and you need to hone all of the parts

✓ Get help – there is so much available on communication skills

✓ Get feedback – communication is about mutual understanding, and feedback on how your communication is received is the only true measure

Further Reading:

Persuasion – the art of influencing people, James Borg, Prentice Hall, 978-0273712992

Knockout Presentations, Diana DiRiesta, Chandler House Press, 978-1886284258

Successful Business Writing, Heather Baker, 978-1532737688

High Impact Presentations, Lee Bowman and Jackie Stewart, Bene Factum Publishing, 978-0952275459

Communicator's Pocketbook, Sean Misteil, 978-1870471411

www.ezinearticles.com

Trait 7:
Open-mindedness

"Renew thyself completely each day; do it again,
and again, and forever again."

Trait 7:
Open-mindedness

In this section we will be:

✓ Defining what being open-minded means

✓ Identifying some of the things that stop us from being open-minded

✓ Examining the effect of negative thinking

✓ Reviewing how habits form

✓ Identifying ways to develop more flexible thinking

✓ Looking at a structured way to help consider other views before reaching a conclusion (PACE technique)

✓ Exploring the importance of seeking feedback on our approach and impact

✓ Listing ways to solicit feedback from others

"An open mind leaves a chance for someone to drop a worthwhile thought in it."

What is open-mindedness?

In this book we have been talking about the traits of people who are truly influential, not people who gain compliance from others through manipulation or force. There is one final trait that influential people share – a willingness to be influenced themselves. It is not enough just to understand the views of others as described in the section on empathy, we also need to be able to adapt, alter or develop our ideas as things change. Influential people do not have a fear of being influenced and this requires open-mindedness. This can be defined as ready to entertain new ideas; an open-minded curiosity or open-minded impartiality.

How open-minded are you?

Let's start by looking at how easy it is to see things differently. The following exercises require you to either think creatively or to find a way to see a different perspective. This is not a test, it is purely a starting point for you to ascertain if this is an area that you need to work on.

Exercise: How open-minded are you?

1. Look at the following image – can you see at least two different perspectives?

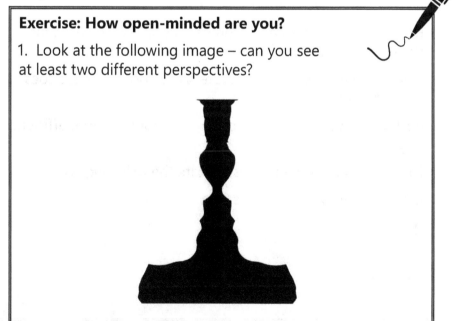

2. When did you last change your mind after listening to someone else's point of view?

....

....

....

3. How readily do you check out your ideas by asking people to challenge them?

....

....

....

4. Have a look at the example below and then complete the next one.

Issue: How do we keep the floor clean?

Restatement 1: How can we prevent people walking on the floor in dirty shoes?

Restatement 2 How can we protect the floor so that it does not get dirty?

Restatement 3 How can we clean the floor in a more efficient way?

Think of three different ways to state the following issue.

Issue: How to make our meetings less boring?

1. ....

2. ....

3. ....

What gets in the way of being open-minded?

Negative thinking

One of the difficulties that research has shown is that when we are presented with a new idea or a challenge:

80% of our first thoughts are negative.

Think about it. That is not 80% of **all** our thoughts, for those of you who consider yourselves to be positive people, but 80% of our **first** thoughts. This is another hard premise for many people to accept. However, it is true that when first faced with a new idea it will probably throw up a whole host of negative thoughts. If we are not careful, those first thoughts can then taint our thinking process and we dive into a negative spiral. This often leads us to point out flaws in ideas rather than looking for anything that could be encouraged. As Peter Drucker has said, "The innovative company understands that innovation starts with an idea, and ideas are somewhat like babies – they are born small, immature and shapeless." Influential people recognise this and are very good at fostering ideas and suggestions even if they are not fully formed.

The tendency to focus on the negative is particularly true when we are facing an area which takes us outside our comfort zone, and many situations in which we need to increase our influence do exactly that. The trick is to understand the process and get past those first negative thoughts by increasing our positive thoughts and creating a positive spiral. One way to do this is to tell yourself that you have to think of three positive things about a new idea before you have earned the right to criticise it.

To recognise the importance of this trait, we only have to consider the other end of the spectrum. We have all experienced the person who delights in "playing devil's advocate" or uses sarcasm or patronising behaviour to dismiss someone else's idea. We also know how much that behaviour reduces that person's ability to really influence us.

Habit

"The only difference between a rut and a grave is depth."

We all form habits and patterns in our behaviour and in our relationships. Sometimes these can make it difficult for us to imagine doing something in a different way. In Robert Winston's book and TV series about the human mind, he used the analogy of a cornfield to describe how these patterns of behaviour develop. If you walk through a cornfield for the first time your footprints will flatten the corn and leave a faint trail. When you come to walk through it again you will probably walk along the same path because it is easier. After the path has been trodden many times, the passage through becomes very clear and easy to follow. It then becomes increasingly difficult to tread a different path. This analogy demonstrates how habits form and how we begin to develop mindsets.

Mindsets are a fixed attitude or disposition that predetermines a person's interpretation of a situation. A classic example of this is stereotyping or pigeon-holing people – at their extreme these mindsets can lead to very destructive attitudes such as racism and sexism.

Other examples include:
✗ Seeing people we work with only in terms of their role within the organisation
✗ Viewing our function or discipline as more important that other people's
✗ Preferring to socialise with the same group of people all the time
✗ Being unwilling to try food we haven't had before

Some of the phrases that may highlight a negative mindset are:
✗ We tried it before
✗ That's not how we do it here
✗ It's impossible
✗ If it is not broken don't mend it
✗ The culture here won't allow that
✗ HR won't like that
✗ That is against the organisation's policy
✗ That's not my job

Sometimes shifting our mindsets about things can enable us to make surprising and powerful changes. Looking at our habits and identifying which work for us and which work against us is the first step to changing unproductive patterns.

However, this is not always easy – if a particular mindset has been developed over many years it can be extremely hard to see things differently.

So how do we ensure that we keep our minds open to change? This has a lot to do with developing flexibility. The more you challenge your mind to see things in different ways the more flexible it becomes.

"The real voyage of discovery consists not in seeing new landscapes but in having new eyes." Marcel Proust

Developing flexible thinking

Exercise: Mind puzzles

The following exercises will help you to see how easy you find it to "think outside the box".

1. Connect all nine dots by drawing four straight continuous lines – (without lifting your pencil or re-tracing a line)

        *   *   *

        *   *   *

        *   *   *

2. Add one straight line to make the following true:

$$5 + 5 + 5 = 550$$

3. Decide where the next two letters of the alphabet should be placed to follow the pattern?

A   E F   H
   B C D   G

4. Identify two things that you have not eaten before and would like to try.

5. In the next two minutes write down all the uses you can think of for a paperclip.

[Ideas for answers are at the back of the book.]

If you found those difficult you may benefit from trying some of the following things – these are all ideas that help to keep our minds flexible.

✓ Doing crosswords, puzzles or Sudoku.
✓ Using brain training software.
✓ Listening to music that is completely different to the music you would normally listen to.
✓ When you do the shopping buy at least two things that are different.
✓ Finding a new way to get to work
✓ Open your mind to other views – think about a controversial issue that you have strong feelings about. Prepare a case defending you opinion with as much evidence as possible. Then prepare another case defending the other side of the argument, again with as much evidence as possible
✓ Spend an hour searching on the internet – start with a topic that interests you and then keep following any links that capture your imagination – keep going and see where it takes you.
✓ Try blocking one of your senses – listen to music with your eyes closed or observe a group of people without being able to hear them.
✓ Play strategy games like chess or bridge or computer strategy games.
✓ Decide to have lunch with different people at work
✓ Read something that you would not normally read.
✓ Visit a museum or art gallery you have not been to before
✓ Watch TV that you would normally avoid – documentary, nature programme, soap, reality show, the news.

Exercise: Developing flexible thinking

Review the list above and identify three things that you are going to do to develop your mind's flexibility.

1. ....
2. ....
3. ....

Considering other viewpoints

PACE technique

This is a useful technique for stopping and thinking about the other person's viewpoint before jumping to conclusions. It involves four stages:

Pause – do not respond immediately, count to 10 before saying anything.

Ask questions – use one of the questions described in the empathy section to help you really understand the other side of the argument. The purpose of asking skilful questions is to really explore someone else's map of the world.
e.g. Tell me more about......
I had not thought of it in that way, please could you give me more detail?
What leads you to that conclusion?

Choose – decide whether the new information means that you want to change your viewpoint. REMEMBER – truly influential people are willing to be influenced.

Engage - respond.

Next time someone is saying something that you disagree with, practise using this technique before you respond.

Seeking feedback

The final part of this trait is an openness to seek, accept and, if necessary, act on feedback from others. The Johari Window is a simple and useful tool for illustrating and helping us to increase our self-awareness. It helps us to understand the importance of both self-disclosure and feedback in developing our self-concept. The Johari Window was developed by psychologists Joseph Luft and Harry Ingham in the 1950s. The name came from combining their first names Joe and Harry.

The model represents information about us as a four paned window. The squares divide personal awareness into four different types as illustrated in the diagram below. The lines between the panes are like window blinds that can move as interaction progresses.

	Known to self	Unknown to self
Known to others	**The Open Area** This area represents information that you know about yourself and that other people know about you. e.g. your name, hair colour, etc.	**The Blind Area** This area represents things that other people know about you that are unknown to you. e.g. your tone of voice, the effect your behaviour has on others etc.
Unknown to others	**The Hidden Area** This area represents the things that you know about yourself but do not share with others.	**The Unknown Area** This is all the information that is currently unknown to you and to others about you. It is the area that is still to be discovered.

The Johari Window panes can be changed in size. To illustrate this further, the diagram below represents an example of the window for a new member to an existing team of people.

	Known to self	**Unknown to self**
Known to others	The Open Area	The Blind Area
Unknown to others	The Hidden Area	The Unknown Area

In this example, the open area is quite small because little is known yet about the new member of the team. Similarly, the blind area is small because other people in the team do not know much about the new person yet.

In our experience, influential people tend to have a larger open area than any other pane. They are constantly striving to increase this area because they recognise that as it grows so does the level of trust and understanding between them and others.

Here are three ways that we can increase the open area of our window:

Through asking others for feedback – this increases the open area by reducing the blind area. Many people find it difficult to give feedback to others, particularly if they have previously been in a relationship or organisation where it was discouraged.

In training workshops, participants have identified the following as some examples of ways they have solicited feedback:

✓ Going through a 360 degree appraisal process

✓ At the end of all one to one meetings with their staff a manager asks the question, "Is there anything I could do that would make your job easier?"

✓ Ask someone before a meeting or presentation if they would be willing to give you some feedback after the event.

✓ Agreeing that during team meetings if someone makes a contribution the rest of the team will give honest feedback.

✓ Through team development workshops

✓ Getting a coach

✓ Finding a mentor

✓ Joining an action learning set

Through self disclosure – being clear and open with people about how we feel, what we want and what we believe in, helps to reduce the hidden area and thereby makes the open area bigger.

This is not about revealing everything about ourselves, as clearly too much information can make others feel uncomfortable. However, it is about being willing to share more of you as a relationship develops.

Through reducing the unknown area – This ties back to some of the suggestions about increasing the flexibility of our mind.

Only by opening ourselves up to new experiences will we discover our potential. Influential people are curious and interested to know what they will discover about themselves through new experiences. That curiosity enables them to move beyond the fear of new experience and into the realms of new possibilities.

In her book, "Feel The Fear and Do It Anyway", Susan Jeffers encourages us to take more risks. We refer to risk taking in the first chapter as being a positive way to increase your influence. This does not refer to taking risks with health and safety, but to taking the kind of risks that help you increase your knowledge of yourself and therefore stretch your mind.

"If you do what you've always done,
you will always get what you've always got."
Anthony Robbins

Exercise: Increasing your open area

Self Disclosure:
Identify 3 things that you are currently keeping to yourself but would like to disclose to someone else in order to deepen your relationship with that person. You can choose either one thing to disclose to 3 separate people or 3 things to disclose to the same person.

Write down what those 3 things are and who you intend to disclose them to.
Think about the benefits,
How will this piece of self-disclosure deepen your relationship with that person/those people?
How will you feel as that relationship improves?

1. ....
2. ....
3. ....

As we discussed earlier, we have more credibility and trust and thus more influence with those people who we have strong relationships with. Keeping your relationships at surface level will decrease rather than increase your influence.

New Experiences:
Identify 3 new experiences that you would like to engage in. These should be things which will take you out of your comfort zone and enable you to understand more about your potential.
Once again consider the benefits.
How will you feel when you try out something new?
What do you believe it will enable you to discover about yourself?

1. ....
2. ....
3. ....

Summary of trait 7: Open-mindedness

In summary, to develop this trait, concentrate on:

- ✓ Practising seeing things from different perspectives
- ✓ Avoiding the trap of responding too quickly to new ideas and therefore being negative
- ✓ Reviewing where your habits and mindsets have formed and checking that they are working for you and not against you
- ✓ Doing things that will help to keep your mind flexible
- ✓ Using the PACE technique to explore other people's views and to allow yourself time to reflect on whether you want to alter your opinion
- ✓ Developing ways to get feedback from other people on your impact and presence

Further Reading:

The Mind Map Book, Tony Buzan and Barry Buzan, BBC Active, 978-1406612790

Feel the Fear and Do It Anyway, Susan Jeffers, Vermillion, 978-0091907075

Triggers, Marshall Goldsmith and Mark Reiter, Profile Books, 978-1781252826,

www.businessballs.com/johariwindowmodel.htm

http://www.forbes.com/sites/davidkwilliams/2013/01/07/the-5-secret-tricks-of-great-people-how-to-become-open-minded-in-2013/#7c9812123bb3

Personal action plan

The purpose of an action plan is twofold; it:

✓ Encourages you to review what you feel you have learned from working through this book

✓ Helps you to commit to some clearly defined actions to transfer those learning points into your everyday life

Action I'm going to take	What is the first step?	When will I take it?

Action I'm going to take	What is the first step?	When will I take it?

Part 2:
A Step by Step Guide to Influencing Effectively

"Success will never be a big step in the future,
success is a small step taken just now."
Jonatan Mårtensson

Introduction to the Six Steps

Effective influencing is the ability to persuade someone to act or behave differently. It is important to recognise that this is not about being tactical – it is not controlling someone or manipulating their behaviour, it is about getting them to move willingly.

True influence is when we gain support and commitment from others by fully explaining our position and taking time to assess their views and needs. It is the ability to achieve our personal objectives whilst building, or at least maintaining, productive working relationships with others.

Our guide to successful influencing is made up of six specific steps. Each of these steps needs to be included. Many people will intuitively use two or three of the steps, however, it is important to follow them all.

The six steps are:

Step 1   Defining what you want

Step 2   Assessing the views of others

Step 3   Defining our influencing power

Step 4   Communicating appropriately

Step 5   Providing space for discussion, questions and feedback

Step 6   Concluding

These steps are significantly easier to execute if you have invested time and effort in developing the traits in part 1 of this book. In each of the steps we provide a reference to the traits which relate to that step and, which once developed, will enhance your ability to navigate this step successfully.

Using this approach will help you to build trust, foster collaborative working relationships and increase your credibility. These are all characteristics that will help you to become a more influential force both at work and at home.

We will take each step in turn, providing explanations and exercises to help you to prepare your case to influence.

Exercise: As a starting point it is useful to write down one specific situation in which you want to influence the outcome - work through the steps with this situation in mind.

I want to influence the following situation:

Step 1: Defining what you want

Effective influencing starts by being clear about what a successful outcome looks like. It is true that we have to begin with the end in mind.

One of the reasons people are ineffective in their influencing is because they have focused on what they don't like or are unhappy about in a situation rather that focusing on what they would like to happen. Many managers will be able to cite examples of people coming to tell them about something they want to change and focusing on all the things they are dissatisfied with. However, when asked the question, 'What would you like to see happen here?' there is no reply.

This demonstrates how weak an influencing position this is - if we don't know what we want how can we expect anyone else to know? It is equally important to be willing to consider whether what you want is possible and reasonable because again, you are unlikely to achieve a successful outcome if your desired outcome is unrealistic.

Relevant traits from part 1

Trait 1 : Knowing What You Want and Believing You Can Achieve It, is the central trait to develop in order to strengthen your capacity to execute step 1 successfully. It is also important to be able to tap into your passion and inspiration at this stage, as this will guide you to what you really want so trait 5 Inspiration is also important.

Exercise: Think about the situation that you would like to influence and ask yourself the following questions:

What do I want to happen?
What would success look like for me?

....

....

....

....

How will that affect other people?

....

....

....

....

How realistic and reasonable is it?

....

....

....

....

What do I not want to happen?

....

....

....

....

Step 2: Assessing the views of others

The next step is about exploring the views of others. Sometimes we limit our ability to influence others successfully by only looking at the issue as we see it and then trying to persuade someone else about the validity of that position. We believe that if we present our ideas clearly and logically, others will follow our suggestions - if this does not happen we begin to try harder by restating the same facts but in a louder voice and with more emphasis. This usually has one of two effects - it either raises resistance in the other person or they 'back down'. This is not true influencing as forced compliance often leads to resentment and bad feeling. If we have to try to influence that person or group again, those feelings will re-emerge.

Therefore, when preparing to influence, it is crucial to explore and understand the perspectives of the people that you are trying to influence as well as appreciating the other factors impacting on the situation. The ability to step away from our personal viewpoint and explore someone else's perception and the wider picture is critical.

The following exercises can help you to do that.

➢ **Walk a mile in my shoes** – this exercise can be used if the situation you are trying to influence involves one or two people.

➢ **Circle of perspectives** – this exercise is useful if the issue that you are trying to change involves influencing a number of different people.

Exercise - Walk a mile in my shoes

Think about the person you are trying to influence. You are going to imagine what the situation looks and feels like from their perspective.

What might the benefits be for them?

....

....

....

....

What problems might they see?

....

....

....

....

What may they possibly be concerned about?

....

....

....

....

What other feelings might they have?

....

....

....

....

What assumptions might you be making about how they perceive the situation?

....

....

....

Exercise - Circle of perspectives

1. In the centre of the circle write your influencing objective.

2. Consider all the people that that you will need to influence if that objective is to be realised and write their names in the segments of the second circle.

3. In the segments in the third circle write what you need or expect from each of those people in relation to your objective.

4. In the outer circle write down what you think their current perspective is on the issue - do you know whether their attitude is positive or negative?

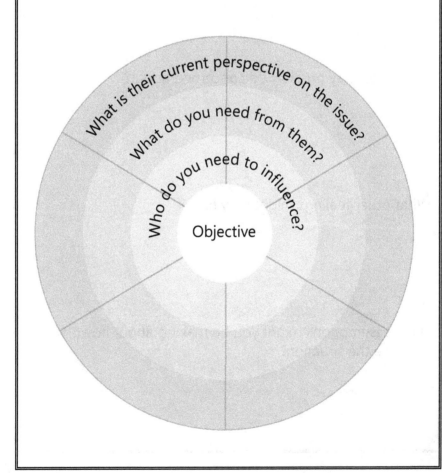

Often we begin by talking to the people we believe will be supportive and leave the 'more difficult' ones until later. However, it is usually more effective to start with the negative people. Firstly they may become more entrenched if they are not spoken to early. Secondly, the sooner that you understand what their resistance is the quicker you can begin to address it. Finally, if they truly have the wrecking power and are not going to be influenced then you may be able to save a lot of time by accepting that on this occasion you are not going to be successful.

Relevant traits from part 1

Trait 4 : Empathy is your fundamental starting point here. You need to be able to step into the world of your stakeholders and developing trait 4 will make this a much easier and more effective process. It is also important to review your credibility with stakeholders at this stage so trait 2 : Credibility is also a very important trait to develop for this step.

Step 3: Defining our influencing power

Once we have considered the views of others we need to assess whether we have any power to influence in this situation.

If we define influence as the process by which we effect a change in someone else's behaviour, then it follows that we may have some power to do that. Effective influencing is the judicious application of our power. Two key things to remember here are:

➢ Power used appropriately is a strong aid to influence and results in commitment, cooperation and acceptance.

➢ Power used inappropriately usually fosters resentment and makes people resistant to being influenced – it may result in compliance but this is not the same as truly influencing.

Power can take many forms. We may agree to do something because we like the person that is asking us or because compelling evidence has been provided that has influenced our thoughts. Over the years, we have worked with thousands of people and have asked them to identify the main reasons they have willingly been influenced. From their responses we have identified eight sources of power.

Position Power

There are many situations in which the underlying capacity we have to influence comes from the position that we hold. This is sometimes referred to as legitimate power and comes when someone is given a role by their organisation or society that has some kind of authority attached to it. Managers in organisations have the right to make reasonable requests of their staff and to expect them to be carried out. Similarly, most people would be influenced by someone in authority, e.g. a police officer asking them to do something.

Hazard Power

This capacity to influence involves outlining risks or consequences to someone in order to persuade them to behave in a different way. Examples of this could be explaining to someone the legal implications of a certain action or letting a colleague know that something contravenes company policy. In a few situations it may be the only power that will influence someone, particularly if the action that you want them to take has no perceived benefit to them personally. People often feel that hazard power is quite a negative source of power, however ,this is not necessarily the case. It is often very effective because the individual you are trying to influence is not aware of the risk or consequence of their behaviour and as soon as it is pointed out they willingly move or change their behaviour.

Expert Power

Sometimes an individual will be able to influence us because we perceive that they have an expertise in a particular area. This expert power may come from their qualifications, skill or experience. A classic example of this occurs when we consult a doctor - we are likely to do what they suggest because we believe they have the knowledge to give us the right advice.

Connection Power

This source of influence is the power that comes from being connected to someone who can exert influence. This is used quite a lot in organisations where the hierarchy is quite flat - so telling someone that you need information from them for a report you are putting together for the Chief Executive is using the power of connection. In many cases it is an important and legitimate source, providing it is true!

Association Power

We are influenced by those we associate with certain qualities that attract us.

This is the foundation of using celebrities to advertise certain products. If we associate someone with success, expertise, prestige, etc. and these are qualities we respect or are attracted to, then we will be influenced by them. Sometimes these are qualities we feel we possess ourselves or qualities which we aspire to. Association power also applies to achievements - if someone has achieved something we admire then we will be influenced by the achievement we associate with that person. This also applies to successful companies. Think of brands such as Disney or Virgin - other companies feel they enhance their chances of success by the association.

Reward Power

Possibly the most straightforward source of influence and the most easily understood.

Influence is exerted through the provision of a tangible reward - this can be financial or a more intrinsic reward such as praise, recognition or visibility. We are influenced by those who can either directly or indirectly provide us with rewards we seek.

The key to reward power is understanding what we personally are able to offer as a reward and understanding what kind of reward is important to the other person.

Personal/Relationship Power

We are influenced by certain people simply because we like them or care about them. This is the power of simply being you and the way that you build relationships. The way in which we behave and use our interpersonal skills is the foundation of this source of influence. It is our own interactions with people and the relationship we have built with them that creates our power to influence them.

Many of us will be influenced by the personal power of those we find charming, trustworthy, friendly, warm, fun, etc.

Information Power

The phrase "knowledge is power" is well known. However, it also has connotations of manipulation, i.e. the hoarding or over-protecting knowledge in order to gain power. Our definition here is different and rests on the fact that the right information to support a case is a very definite source of influence.

The emphasis must be on gaining the right information and using it appropriately. A good example is "we are losing 300 days a year through sickness" as a supporting piece of information for influencing a case around better support for the health and well-being of staff.

The right power, used appropriately, is the key to how easily and effectively you will be able to influence in a situation. Unfortunately, many people see exerting power as a negative thing because they have observed the manipulative application of it rather than it being used positively.

Exercise - Go back to your influencing objective and ask yourself these three questions:

Which powers are most appropriate to use with this group or individual?

....
....
....
....
....

If I currently do not have any power with this group or individual, which source could I develop?

....
....
....
....
....

What might they be concerned about?

....
....
....
....
....
....

Relevant traits from part 1

Trait 2 : Credibility and trait 4 : Trustworthiness are really important traits to assist you at this stage. This is probably the step where there are possible temptations towards manipulation, so it's really important to ensure that you maintain your credibility and trustworthiness while exercising your influencing power. It will certainly pay off in the long run.

Step 4:
Communicating
appropriately

You can prepare well and take into consideration all the previous steps and still forget that HOW you communicate your case is crucial.

There are 3 main things to consider. Your case needs to be communicated in a way which is:

➢ Compelling

➢ Credible

➢ Understandable

Compelling - this relates back to your understanding of the other person's or people's perspectives and your ability to articulate the benefit to them.

Credible - providing the right information; not just the facts but information relating to the source of power that you identified in step 3.

Understandable - this relates to your ability to be clear and congruent. It is key to clearly state what you hope to achieve and to show empathy in the way you communicate. The congruence comes from ensuring that you match your words, tone of voice and body language in order to avoid giving a mixed message.

The following framework can help you to prepare your communication:

Introduce the issue

➢ Set the scene and the context - including what you want to achieve and how you will work together.
➢ It is important to express, right at the start, that the influencing process is a two way process.

An example of a good introduction is:

'I'd like to see if we can reach a better understanding about how we are going to work together to manage the monthly returns.'

Acknowledge all perspectives - your own and the other person(s)

'I appreciate that this is very important to you..........'
'I am aware that this change will present challenges for all of us.'
'I know this is going to be a very big upheaval for your department.'

Outline the agenda - what you will be covering.

Provide the compelling reasons for your case - remember these must provide a benefit for the other person/people.

Offer a space for discussion and questions (see step 5)

Relevant traits from part 1

Trait 6 : Strong Communication Capability is clearly essential for this step. Continually focusing on your ability to communicate exceptionally well over all modalities is a critical part of influencing. However, at this stage trait 1 comes back into play as you need to be very clear about what you want, and this needs to be balanced with trait 4 : Empathy, which is predominant in determining our capacity to influence. Harnessing your inspiration and passion and expressing that to the person(s) you wish to influence is also central, so trait 5 is key. You will also need to establish your trustworthiness and credibility so traits 2 and 3 become equally valuable. As you can see, this is the point at which 6 of the traits converge, and the ease you feel with each of them will greatly contribute to your success at this stage.

Step 5: Provide space for discussion, questions and feedback

It is very easy, once you have presented your case, to be so convinced of its essential rightness that you don't want further discussion, you simply want agreement!

Remember that most people presented with something new need time to process their thinking and ask questions for clarification. This is not to be construed as rejection or negativity, but needs to be seen as part of the natural process of influencing.

It is important to recognise that we need patience at this stage of influencing, as rushing may prevent you from succeeding. Patience, it is said, is a virtue and never more so than when we are at this stage of our influencing process.

The more open you are to discussion at this point, the more chance you will have of influencing the final outcome. Your openness needs to be genuine - remember it is very likely that the perspectives presented will be valid and also someone may have a point that you have completely missed.

Here are some examples of insightful questions that you can use to help explore the other person's point of view:
"What are your main concerns?"
"Tell me more about what is concerning you?"
"How do you think this will impact on you/us/our customers?"
"What do you think is the best way of implementing this change?"
"What do you think are our options?"
"How do you think we can move forward"?

This step is about looking for common ground and there are some simple dos and don'ts that can really help.

Do	Don't
Let the other person speak	Interrupt
Listen	Get defensive
Be understanding of concerns	Switch off
Actively look for common ground	Just keep repeating your point of view
Be prepared to compromise	Give up
Use insightful questions to draw out their concerns	

Don't Get Defensive

It is worth saying a final word about defensiveness. Defensiveness is a very natural reaction when we feel we need to justify our point of view, but it almost never has the desired effect. Defensiveness will derail an influencing process quicker than anything else, so it is really important to try and avoid this pitfall. Continuing to use empathy without giving up will be much more effective. For example: "I know this is a big upheaval and I want to support you as much as possible. I am also feeling the challenges, and I think if we all discuss our concerns it will really help."

If you can stay open-minded and provide a genuine space for discussion and feedback, you will be giving yourself the best chance for a good outcome to your influencing.

Relevant traits from part 1

Trait 7 : Open-Mindedness is your principal focus for this step. Developing a truly open-mind strengthens your ability to influence with integrity and avoid manipulation. You will still need your communication capability at this stage and your empathy, so traits 6 and 4 are equally relevant. Whether or not the person or people you are looking to influence trust you is also paramount at this stage, so the development of trait 3 will greatly strengthen your capacity to execute this step successfully.

Step 6:
Concluding

Our final step sounds very obvious, but is another commonly missed part of the process. Once you have discussed the options and come to some form of conclusion, it is really important to establish clearly, exactly what has or has not been agreed and what follow up actions will be necessary.

There are 3 potential conclusions to the influencing process:-

➤ Full agreement has been reached

➤ Partial agreement has been reached

➤ Agreement has not been reached

All require different strategies at this point.

If full agreement has been reached

➤ Summarise exactly what has been agreed

➤ Decide what the next steps will be and who will be responsible for any actions

➤ Agree if you need any follow up meetings/conversations in order to progress and, if so, when these will be

➤ Confirm all of this by written communication like email so that all parties have the agreement in writing

If partial agreement has been reached

➤ Summarise exactly what has been agreed AND what has not been agreed

If the compromise reached is sufficient and you do not need to revisit any areas in which you have disagreed, then follow the process exactly as if full agreement has been reached.

➤ Decide what the next steps will be and who will be responsible for any actions

➤ Agree if you need any follow up meetings/conversations in order to progress and, if so, when these will be

➤ Confirm all of this by written communication like email so that all parties have the agreement in writing

If the compromise reached is a good initial outcome but you need to revisit any of the areas in which you have not agreed, then you need to decide how you will revisit these.

It may be that one of you has to do some further fact finding, it may be that you need to talk to other people, it may be that you are waiting on the outcome of some other process.

Whatever is going to happen next, you need to:-

➤ Agree on any follow up actions and who will be responsible for them

➤ Agree at what point those actions will be completed

➤ Set a date to come back together to discuss the next steps

➤ Confirm all of this by written communication like email so that all parties have the agreement in writing

If no agreement has been reached

➢ Decide on whether you can or cannot leave it like this and state very clearly whether you will continue to pursue this matter

➢ Agree if anyone else needs to be consulted

➢ Always keep the door open for further discussion

Examples of ways to keep the door open:-

"Lets both take time to review our options and see if we can think of any ideas that will help us move forward. How about if we meet again next week when we have both had a chance to think?"

"I think we have raised a lot of important issues today and at least we are clear on what the areas of concern are. Maybe if we talk again in a few days we can come up with some ideas that will help us resolve some of those concerns."

"I will have a chat to .... and then get back to you and let you know how they feel. In the meantime, if there is any more information I can get for you that will help please let me know."

➢ Finally, again confirm by email what you are doing and how you intend to move forward.

Relevant traits from part 1

As we say at the beginning of this step – this is a commonly missed, yet absolutely vital part of the process, and you will need to draw again on your ability to communicate clearly AND with empathy to close well, so traits 6 and 4 are once again central to concluding successfully. You will also be drawing on your credibility and trustworthiness, so traits 2 and 3 are still essential here. You will need to refer back to your starting point for clarity so the stronger you feel around trait 1 : Knowing What You Want and Believing You Will Achieve It will help you immensely with your clarity about what stage you are at. Remember to draw on trait 7 : Open-Mindedness if you have only reached partial agreement or no agreement as you will need to regroup.

If, as hoped, your influencing has come to a successful conclusion, remember to revisit trait 5 : Inspiration – you will need to bring this forth in order to implement your successful conclusion effectively.

Conclusion to the steps

Michelangelo famously quoted that "Genius is infinite patience," and the same could be said of influencing!

We know from experience that if you follow the six steps to influencing you are giving yourself the best chance of a positive outcome. However, that does not mean to say that you will succeed immediately. It is so important that you are prepared to have patience if you do not achieve your goals in the very first instance. One of the most important Don'ts we mention in Step 5 is Don't Give Up. If you believe you have a strong case, you may have to follow the process several times in order to finally succeed.

Remember that you will be presenting ideas that you have thought through but the person or people you are trying to influence are coming fresh to your ideas and will need time to think, particularly if what you are asking for has a significant impact on them.

If you are prepared to be patient, keep the door open and keep revisiting the steps as necessary, you will significantly increase your chance of influencing successfully.

The Six Steps Case Study One

Charlotte came to a coaching session despairing about the way her monthly management meetings were going. She did not chair them herself and so felt completely powerless to do anything to improve them. When asked to describe a typical meeting she said that she felt the whole thing was a total waste of time for several reasons. Firstly, the meeting was dominated by three very overbearing members of the team who argued constantly. The agenda was never completed because people went off at tangents and the chair did not control the time. No actions were agreed at the end of each item and the whole experience was extremely frustrating.

Step 1 - Defining what you want

Charlotte was asked what a successful outcome would look like. What would she like to see happen? She identified the following as the ideal outcome:

➤ The meeting limited to two hours - starting and finishing on time

➤ Realistic agenda

➤ Well chaired to ensure even contribution

➤ Clear actions recorded and completed

Step 2 - Assessing the views of others

We then completed the circle of perspectives to see who would need to be influenced and to consider their current position. This exercise highlighted that the influencing process needed to start with the chair as most of the issues revolved around the meeting not having a clear enough focus and this could be achieved through better agenda production and management.

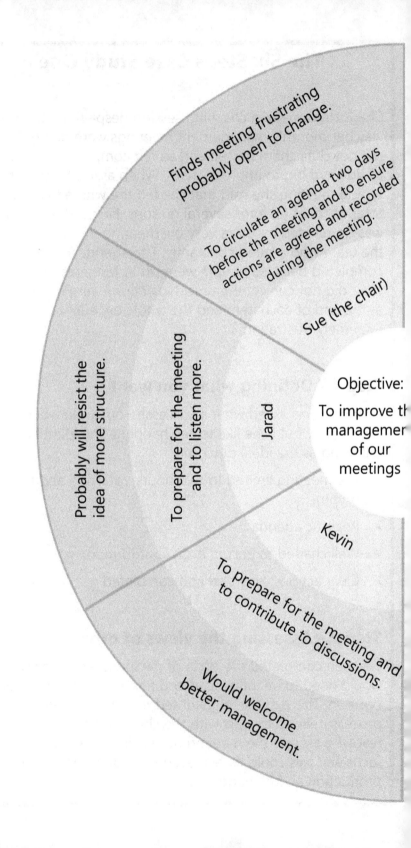

Finds meeting frustrating probably open to change.

To circulate an agenda two days before the meeting and to ensure actions are agreed and recorded during the meeting.

Sue (the chair)

Probably will resist the idea of more structure.

To prepare for the meeting and to listen more.

Jarad

Objective:
To improve th management of our meetings

Kevin

To prepare for the meeting and to contribute to discussions.

Would welcome better management.

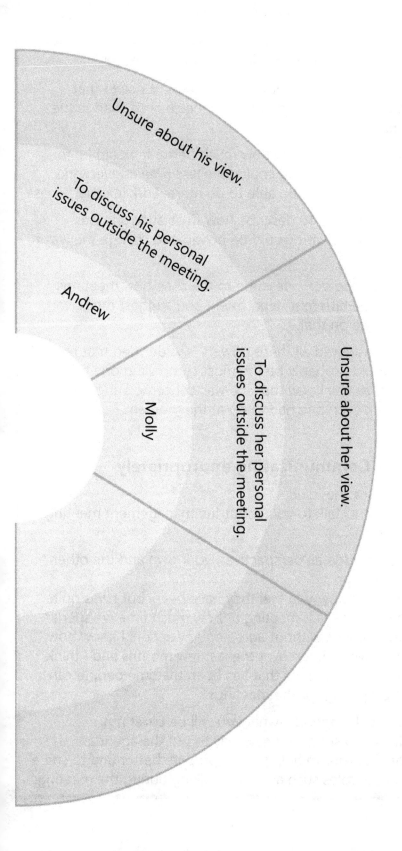

Unsure about his view.

To discuss his personal issues outside the meeting.

Andrew

Molly

To discuss her personal issues outside the meeting.

Unsure about her view.

163

Step 3 - Defining our influencing power

Charlotte identified a number of sources of power that she could use to try and influence the chair to change the meeting.

Reward power - outline how much better it would be for everyone if the meeting could take less time as everyone would gain time and be able to do more work in other areas.

Personal power - to describe how frustrating she was finding it and ask if it would be possible to change the way it was run.

Association power - describe to the chair how meetings were run in a different department and suggest modelling their practice on that.

Having considered all these powers, she decided that reward power would probably be the most compelling one for Sue (the chair) as she knew that she was concerned about how much work everyone had to do at the moment.

Step 4 - Communicating appropriately

➤ Introduce the issue.
'I would like to talk to you about the management meeting last week.'

➤ Acknowledge all perspectives, your own and the other person(s).
'I am not sure how you feel they have been, but I was quite frustrated at the last meeting at how much time we spent discussing things without agreeing any action. I know how busy we have all been over the last few months and I think one of the casualties of that has been the time people can give to preparing for the meetings.'

➤ Outline the agenda (what you will be covering).
'I would like to suggest a new way to put the agenda together in order to help people prepare better and to share some of the roles such as minute taking during the meeting.'

> Provide the compelling reasons for your case (remember these must provide a benefit for the other person/people).

'Hopefully this will save time for all of us and stop all the administrative burden falling on you.'

> Offer a space for discussion and questions (Step 5).

'How does that sound to you?'

Step 5 - Providing for discussion, questions and feedback

Despite being slightly defensive to begin with, Sue quickly recognised that this was not an attack on her but a genuine desire to improve the situation for everyone. The discussion that followed focused on the practical things that could be done to achieve the desired outcome and was productive and valuable.

Step 6 - Concluding

> Summarise exactly what has been agreed.

Charlotte and Sue agreed that the meeting was not achieving as much as it could and that it would be something that would be discussed at the next meeting.

> Decide what the next steps will be and who will be responsible for any actions.

Sue agreed to circulate an agenda 48 hours before the next meeting and to make one of the agenda items – 'Ways to make this meeting more productive.'

Charlotte offered to take the minutes at the next meeting.

> Confirm all of this by email so that all parties have the agreement in writing.

After the discussion, Charlotte sent an email to Sue thanking her for her time and confirming the actions they had agreed.

The Six Steps Case Study Two

A client came to a coaching session with the following influencing issue. He managed in a customer service environment where many of the customers had difficulty accessing their services between 9-5. There was already some flexible opening which included opening at 8.30 am and one night a week staying open until 7 pm. It was proposed that these opening times should be increased to opening at 8 am and staying open 4 nights a week until 7 pm. This meant that the working patterns of the staff had to be changed and this was causing a lot of problems. There had already been one staff meeting which was very turbulent and no agreement had been reached. It was very important for the client to influence the staff over this issue. He could simply implement the new system and bulldoze over the resistance (and at one point this was the only option he could see). However, this would fail in its key objective of giving better service to the customer if staff were angry and resentful. We worked on identifying his steps to presenting his case.

Step 1 - Defining what you want

The client was asked what a successful outcome would look like. What would he like to see happen? He identified the following as his ideal outcome:-

➤ The new system was implemented within the month
➤ Staff agreed that it was both necessary and the best way forward for the customers
➤ Staff worked together on how to manage the new working patterns and these were realistic and workable
➤ Anger and resentment were replaced by commitment and enthusiasm

The client identified that the key people to influence were the staff who would need to change their working patterns.

Step 2 - Assessing the views of others

We used the circle of perspectives on the staff involved and looked at them as individuals rather than one group (see next page).

The manager identified that he needed the same things from each individual, but their perspectives were varied so one approach would not work for everyone. It also helped him to start to understand their perspectives and how his own approach and lack of understanding had raised the initial resistance.

Step 3 - Defining our influencing power

The manager realised he had a number of sources of power in this situation: position power as he did have the authority to insist on the change, hazard power as this change could help to prevent job losses and reduction of service in the future, reward power in terms of giving the staff the opportunity to influence their personal rota patterns. He decided that the most appropriate were reward and judicious use of hazard power. Interestingly he felt that although he had position power this would not give him the result he wanted.

Step 4 - Communicating appropriately

We talked through the options for communicating in this situation. Discussion and feedback would be needed, and exploring how individuals felt and understanding their different perspectives was far more important than speed. He decided that the most appropriate method to use was face to face meetings with individuals.

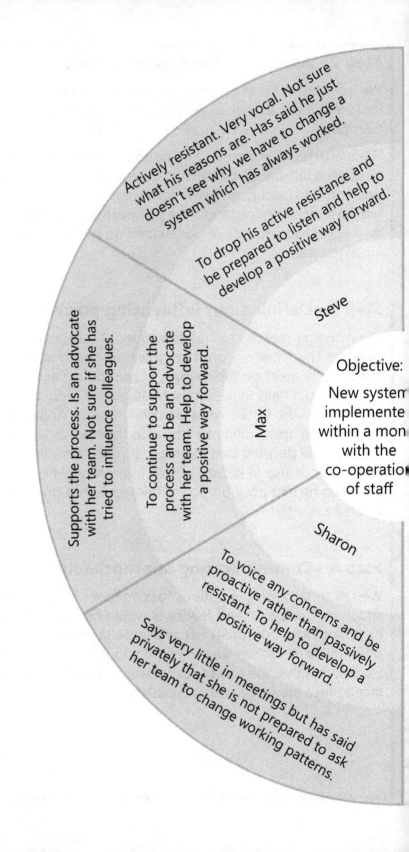

Actively resistant. Very vocal. Not sure what his reasons are. Has said he just doesn't see why we have to change a system which has always worked.

To drop his active resistance and be prepared to listen and help to develop a positive way forward.

Steve

Supports the process. Is an advocate with her team. Not sure if she has tried to influence colleagues.

To continue to support the process and be an advocate with her team. Help to develop a positive way forward.

Max

Objective:

New system implemente within a mon with the co-operatio of staff

Sharon

To voice any concerns and be proactive rather than passively resistant. To help to develop a positive way forward.

Says very little in meetings but has said privately that she is not prepared to ask her team to change working patterns.

Understands reasons for change but is adamant that her child care arrangements will not allow her to change her working pattern.

To drop her active resistance and be prepared to listen and help to develop a positive way forward.

Lucy

Ciaran

To voice his support openly for the process and not just to me. Help to develop a positive way forward.

Has said privately that he supports the process. Does not voice his support in meetings.

Gaynor

To drop her passive resistance and refrain from conversations which encourage others to actively resist. To help to develop a positive way forward.

Is sulky and silent in meetings and has lots of "corner" conversations with Steve. I think she is making bullets for him to fire.

We then developed a scripted opening following the communication framework which he could use with everyone:-

"Hi, thanks very much for giving me some time today. I have had time now to think about the meeting regarding the new opening hours and wanted to discuss all the concerns that were raised. I know that everyone's perspective on this is different, so I thought it was important to talk to you all individually to make sure I don't miss anything important.

I am committed to implementing the new system within the next month. However, I am also committed to dealing with as many of your concerns as possible and to discuss any major problems this may cause for you.

I would really like us to discuss your views today and see if we can reach a better understanding about how this might work.

Is that OK by you?"

This opening allowed him to set the scene, introduce the context, state clearly what his goal was but also start to show empathy about the concerns and problems this might cause.

He then went on to speak first about the potential concerns that the individual may have, e.g.

"I understand that this may impact on your childcare arrangements and could cause you some difficulties. Will you tell me about that?"

He then allowed the members of staff to express their concerns and simply listened until he was sure that he fully understood the situation before moving into any solutions.

When he did start to discuss solutions he firstly reinforced the benefits using his power to influence, but also confirmed his understanding of the staff's personal concerns. e.g.

"I think I understand your situation now but please tell me if I have got any of this wrong. I feel as if you understand that this will benefit all of us in terms of giving us all more

flexibility and make our customers happier and will also make sure we can keep this location open rather than having to join with the central site, but your main problem is still your need to be able to collect your children by 6.30 on Tuesdays and Thursdays - is that right?"

He then went on to ask for input and ideas while continuing to make sure he did not give the impression of backing off from his goal.

"What ideas do you have on how we could implement this system and make it work for you?"

He then opened up step 5 for discussion and feedback.

Step 5 – Providing space for discussion, questions and feedback

We talked about the fact that he should still expect quite a lot of discussion and probably still resistance and negativity, and he needed to actively support people to express their views and manage it rather than take it personally and start to defend his position which would put him back to square one.

This part of the conversation cannot be scripted as it is impossible to know what others will say. To give himself time to think if he started getting frustrated, we rehearsed some phrases he could use in the conversation, e.g.

"I really understand your concerns. How can we move forward here?"
"What are your ideas at this point about our options",
"Let me check that I have understood your main concerns....................."

The key thing is to keep focused on the ultimate outcome, but keep the conversation as a genuine discussion rather than allowing it to become defensive.

For this particular manager's staff, these conversations felt so different from their previous interactions that it took a little time for them to feel confident that the manager did want to hear their views and he had to work quite hard in the discussions to stay empathic. However, it produced huge dividends. Once people genuinely felt his empathy they started to drop their resistance and come up with options. After he had seen everyone individually, he called another staff meeting at which he fed back the ideas people had come up with in the one to ones and invited a free discussion on which ideas would work best. Everyone (including himself) was much less defensive than they had been previously and they worked out rotas to suit people's individual needs as far as possible and made sure that shifts which caused real problems were kept to a minimum. E.g. the woman whose childcare had been an issue was, with the co-operation of her colleagues, able to structure most of her shifts around her husband's work pattern. It only meant her paying for 2 extra childcare hours per month which she was happy with.

The manager achieved his aim of implementing the new system with a spirit of co-operation rather than conflict.

Step 6 – Concluding

Individual conversations followed different patterns and the manager made sure that he closed off each individual meeting with a summary of what had been agreed which was backed up by email confirmation. As a staff meeting was to follow each of the individual conversations, all of these fell into the partial agreement box, as until the staff meeting had taken place, it was impossible to have full agreement.

Following the individual conversations therefore:-

Summarise what has and has not been agreed and decide on the next steps

> Each of the members of the team agreed to write up their ideas and forward them to the manager to be put forward for discussion with everyone at the staff meeting.

> The manager acknowledged receipt of these and prepared an agenda for the staff meeting including everyone's ideas for discussion.

Summarise what has been agreed and confirm it in writing

After the staff meeting there was full agreement and the exact agreements were confirmed as part of the new rota so that everyone was clear about what had been agreed.

Decide on next steps and confirm in writing

There was also an agreement to review the system after 8 weeks to make sure it was working and iron out any problems. The manager asked his secretary to co-ordinate this meeting and emailed everyone to inform them of the date, venue and time. He also issued a paper with questions such as:-

What has worked well now we have implemented the new rota? What problems have you encountered?

If you have encountered problems what are your ideas for how we could solve these problems? What feedback have you had from our customers?

These helped to focus people on what they were discussing in the next meeting.

Overall outcome

The manager achieved his aim of implementing the new system with a spirit of co-operation rather than conflict.

NOTES:

Final Thoughts

We hope you have enjoyed your journey through the 7 traits and the 6 steps to influencing and will feel able to start to practise them in your life from here.

You will already be in possession of some of the traits and feel confident with some of the steps and will want to strengthen others. Please continue to use the exercises and the additional references to expand your understanding and as a starting point to further skill development.

Be patient with yourself. One of the most important things in self-development is to allow yourself the time to learn.

Our experience is that becoming more influential is a development journey and we hope that we have given you a pathway to guide you on that journey.

We feel privileged to share our views with you through this book and please contact us if you have questions or feel our work would help you in other ways.

You can find us on

www.loisburton.co.uk

www.deborahdalley.com

Best Wishes

Lois and Deborah

ACTIONS:

Answers to the mind puzzles in Trait 7:

The following exercises will help you to see how easy you find it to "think outside the box".

1. Connect all nine dots by drawing four straight continuous lines – (without lifting your pencil or re-tracing a line)

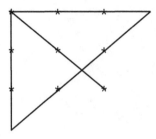

2. You could make the equals sign into not equals:

$$5 + 5 + 5 \neq 550$$

or (there is usually more than one solution) make the first plus into a 4 so the equation reads 545 +5

$$5 \,4\, 5 + 5 = 550$$

3. The top row have all straight lines, the bottom letters have curves.

<u>A   E F H I   </u>
  B C D   G   J

4. When are you going to try the two foods you chose?

5. Here are just a few ideas for using a paperclip:

Open a letter
Replace a zip
Unclog a tube of glue
As a wire in an electric circuit
As an earring
As a weight
To pull a fish along in magnetic fishing game
To pick a lock
To keep your hair in place
As a tooth pick
Clean your nails
Scratch your name on a rock
As money (stranger things have been used)
As a fish hook
Make a hole in something
Melt it down and make a key (a very small one)
What if the paper clip was plastic....
What if it were giant sized and then you melted it - you could make loads of stuff

You could even use it to hold paper together!

How to Develop Your Assertive Communication

UK Spelling
Deborah Dalley
UK: 978-1539391555
World: 978-1537637723

This book will provide you with the tools and techniques to become a more assertive communicator. It is full of practical tips, case studies and exercises. These will build your skills and change the way you communicate to help you achieve your goals.

Discover how to:

- ✓ Recognise different forms of behaviour and identify your dominant behaviour type
- ✓ Find ways to develop your confidence in a range of situations
- ✓ Manage the anxiety associated with handling stressful encounters
- ✓ Use the right words, tone and body language to be assertive
- ✓ Communicate confidently when you want to say no, raise an awkward issue, stand your ground or disagree with someone
- ✓ Prepare for challenging conversations
- ✓ Manage your own and others emotions during difficult encounters

Over 31 practical ideas to help you learn to communicate assertively

"I always imagined that other people just knew how to deal with difficult situations, I now believe that with practice anyone can manage it."

"The book has opened my eyes. I feel empowered and ready to take responsibility for my life."

"I thought this book was excellent, readable and easy to work through."

CPSIA information can be obtained
at www.ICGtesting.com
Printed in the USA
LVHW041531210323
742169LV00009B/903